CW00432262

# DISCOVERING
# ANCIENT IRELAND

# DISCOVERING ANCIENT IRELAND

KELLI ANN MALONE

*To Mom and Dad, Jay, Meri and wee Victor.*

First published 2010

The History Press Ireland
119 Lower Baggot Street
Dublin 2
Ireland
www.thehistorypress.ie

© Kelli Ann Malone, 2010

The right of Kelli Ann Malone to be identified as the Author
of this work has been asserted in accordance with the
Copyrights, Designs and Patents Act 1988.

All rights reserved. No part of this book may be reprinted
or reproduced or utilised in any form or by any electronic,
mechanical or other means, now known or hereafter invented,
including photocopying and recording, or in any information
storage or retrieval system, without the permission in writing
from the Publishers.

British Library Cataloguing in Publication Data.
A catalogue record for this book is available from the British Library.

ISBN 978 1 8458 8977 7

Typesetting and origination by The History Press
Printed in Great Britain
Manufacturing managed by Jellyfish Print Solutions Ltd

# CONTENTS

Acknowledgements      6

Glossary      7


one      Discovering Ancient Ireland      15

two      Paleolithic and Mesolithic (700000–4000 BCE)      21

three      The Neolithic (4000–2000 BCE)      30

four      The Bronze Age (2200–500 BCE)      74

five      The Iron Age (500 BCE– AD 500)      98


Bibliography      125

# ACKNOWLEDGEMENTS

Thank you to Tyler Brown, proof-reader extraordinaire; The History Press Ireland, for taking this project on; Champlain College Dublin, especially Stephen Robinson, for keeping me employed while I worked on this book; Jessica Guertin for her photographs of Oweynagat Cave; Kevin Griffin and Pat Dargan at the Dublin Institute of Technology for being colleagues and mates; all the caretakers of Ireland's past; Iggy the Magic Cat; and to Lesley for everything else that matters.

# GLOSSARY

**Acheulean Hand Axe:** a large, hand-held cutting tool common to the Paleolithic which is often pear-shaped or oval, with a sharp point, and hammer-like butt.

**Band:** the most simple form of human social organisation. Band societies usually consist of twenty to fifty kin-related people, who are egalitarian and have informal leadership.

**Bann Flake:** a diagnostic stone artefact of the Irish Mesolithic Period.

**Barrow:** typically earth and/or rubble mound used to enclose single or multiple burials. Also referred to as a 'tumulus' or 'cairn' (when the structure is principally of stone).

**Beaker:** a simple, clay drinking-vessel without handles, which are commonly found in graves in the Bronze Age; beaker vessels are often related to the Beaker People, an archaeological culture who flourished during the Bronze Age in Europe.

**Boulder burial:** a burial feature in which the burial(s) are covered with a large central boulder. In Ireland, boulder burials are often associated with stone circles.

**Bowl barrow:** small, round, burial mounds surrounded by a ditch; common throughout the Bronze Age and into the Iron Age.

**Bronze Age:** a period in Europe which lasts from *c.* 2500 BCE to 750 BCE and is related to the introduction and use of bronze into the tool-kit. In Ireland, the Bronze Age is generally recognised as lasting from *c.* 2200/2000 BCE to about 500/400 BCE when iron begins to be introduced.

**Brú na Bóinne:** Irish meaning Place of the Boyne. Generally the location of Newgrange, Knowth, and Dowth, and forty or more additional, lesser-known sites near the Boyne River in County Meath, Ireland.

**Cairn:** a predominantly stone burial mound.

**Carrowkeel pottery:** a crude, thick-walled pottery of the Irish Neolithic, associated with the Megalithic cemetery of Carrowkeel in County Sligo.

**Chalcolithic:** literally *copper-stone age*. A transitional period between the late Neolithic and Early Bronze Age when copper was first introduced.

**Chert:** a fine-grained sedementary rock also known as flint.

**Chiefdom:** a social organisation with clear social ranking, varying degrees of centralisation, and defined leadership. A chiefdom typically encompasses several villages or communities under the control of a single paramount chief.

**Clochan:** a dry-stone hut, dating from the Middle Ages; in use in Ireland since the Bronze Age, but most often associated with monastic sites.

**Court tomb:** a Neolithic-period tomb, characterised by a dry-stone burial chamber with an adjoining walled open court.

**Cruciform:** when used in relation to passage tombs, a cruciform shape with an elongated passageway leading to central chamber, with three smaller chambers to the right, left, and forward.

**Cursus:** a late Neolithic or Bronze Age earthwork characterised by long, parallel banks, often with inner or outer ditches, and thought to be a processional way. The Banqueting Hall at the Hill of Tara is likely a cursus which led to the *Ráith na Ríg*.

**Debitage:** waste flakes, spalls, and other debris created in the manufacture of stone tools.

**Dolmen:** a Neolithic-period tomb consisting of two or more upright stones with a large capstone. In Ireland examples include the Poulnabrone dolmen and the Proleek dolmen. Also known as a portal tomb or portal dolmen.

**Dolmen circle:** a stone circle enclosing a portal dolmen.

**Drumlin:** a smooth, oval hill deposited and shaped by glacial drift.

**Earthen enclosure:** a Neolithic or Bronze Age earthwork surrounded by a circular, oval, or elliptical bank; some may also have an interior or exterior fosse. The enclosed area may have been used for burials, houses, or to hold animals.

**Earthwork:** any earthen embankment, often used as a form of fortification.

**Egalitarian:** non-stratified society, with little or no concept of social hierarchy, political or economic status, class or a permanent form of leadership. In Ireland, Mesolithic hunter-gatherer society is thought to have been egalitarian.

**Esker ridge:** a long ridge of stratified glacial gravel. In Ireland, the *Eiscer Riada* is a long series of esker ridges which run nearly contiguously from Dublin to Galway. In ancient times, it is believed the series of esker ridges in Ireland may have served as a form of 'highway', enabling people to cross the countryside while avoiding marshy and boggy areas.

**Excarnation:** the process of leaving a body to the elements to decay prior to burial or cremation.

**Flint knapping:** the shaping of stone into tools through the use of hammer stones and other devises.

**Fosse:** a ditch or moat surrounding a fortification.

**Fulacht fiadh:** an Irish term which refers to a particular horseshoe-shaped burnt-mound believed to have been used for cooking or brewing during the Bronze Age.

**Geophysical survey:** in archaeology, the use of ground-penetrating radar, magnetometers, and other devices, to discern underground or otherwise invisible features on the landscape.

**Gneiss:** a coarse, grained, metamorphic rock similar to granite.

**Gorget:** a protective covering for the throat often in the form of a metal collar.

**Grave goods:** objects buried with a body.

**Hallstatt:** the Early Iron Age in Europe (*c.* 750 BCE-400 BCE), named for the site of Hallstatt in the Salzkammergut in Austria.

**Hectare:** 2.47 acres or 10,000 square metres.

**Henge:** a roughly circular, or oval-shaped, flat area, encircled or enclosed by an earthwork that usually is made of a ditch and external bank. Most henges have either a single ditch or a pair of concentric ditches.

**Hoard:** archaeologically, the term is a deliberate deposit of objects, which are buried for future use or recovery. The objects can be whole, broken, or destroyed in some manner. Hoarding of objects was common during the Bronze Age in Ireland (e.g., the Dowris Hoard). Hoards could be votive offerings.

**Holocene:** the current inter-glacial, geological epoch.

**Hominid:** the biological family that includes *Homo sapiens*, *Neanderthals*, and other forerunners of modern humans.

**Horticulture:** archaeologically, the cultivation of gardens.

**Iron Age:** the final technological and cultural phase in the Three-Age System of Stone-Bronze-Iron Ages, when iron largely replaced bronze in the human tool kit. The Iron Age began at various times throughout Asia, the Middle East, and Europe. In Ireland, the Iron Age began quite late, with iron artefacts only becoming common in the archaeological record in the first and second centuries BCE. (See Hallstatt and La Tene)

**Kerb stone:** archaeologically, the large, flat stones used to delimit and support burial tombs, such as Newgrange, Knowth, and Dowth. In many cases kerb stones are highly decorated.

**La Tene:** the Late Iron Age period named for the site on Lac Neuchatal in Switzerland known for its distinctive artefacts and stylised artwork.

**LiDAR (Light Detection and Ranging):** an optical, remote sensing technology, used archaeologically as a method of reading the landscape in detail. LiDAR has the ability to cut through vegetation to expose landscape features that may otherwise not be visible to the eye.

**Lintel:** a horizontal beam or stone that spans an opening, or is used to join two uprights in an architectural structure.

**Lunula:** a crescent-shaped decorative collar; in Ireland during the Bronze Age lunulae were usually of gold, and could be incised with intricate decoration. Lunula-shaped carvings are also visible on many kerb stones and uprights, such as at Knowth in County Meath.

**Megafauna:** archaeologically used to refer to large-bodied mammals, who weigh in excess of 45kgs. During the end of the Pleistocene, many megafauna (who could be massive, weighing up to 4500kgs) experienced extinction, due to changes in climate and environment.

**Megalith:** literally large stone. Archaeologically a class of monument using large stones as the structural base, including stone circles, some henge monuments, passage tombs, and standing stones.

**Mesolithic:** literally 'middle Stone Age'. Archaeologically, the period succeeding the Pleistocene, characterised by small, highly mobile, kin-related bands. Mesolithic peoples in Ireland followed seasonal migrations of herd animals, and exploited local resources.

**Microlith:** literally small stone. Microliths are a class of stone tool commonly associated with the mesolithic era.

**Neanderthal:** a type of hominid, which inhabited parts of the world, including Europe, from about 100,000 to 30,000 years ago. Modern humans and Neanderthals shared a common ancestor about 500,000 years ago.

**Neolithic:** literally 'new Stone Age'. The time period following the Mesolithic, characterised by the development of agriculture, settled communities, pottery, megaliths, passage tombs and other stone burial chambers, and marked territories. Neolithic peoples were aware of cosmological changes and are believed to have practised complex religious rituals.

**Óenach:** an Irish term relating a seasonal gathering or gathering place such as the Tailteann Óenach in County Meath.

**Orthostat:** an upright stone; used in relation to an architectural structure.

**Paleolithic:** literally old Stone Age. The time period ranging from the first tool-using hominids (approx. 2.5million years ago), to the beginning of the Mesolithic period. Current archaeology indicates that humans did not inhabit Ireland during the Paleolithic.

**Palynology:** the scientific study of pollens.

**Passage tomb:** a burial chamber with at least one passageway leading to a single or more central chamber. Usually constructed of stone with a turf covering. Most common during the Neolithic period in Ireland.

**Pastoralism:** the subsistence method related to the domestication of herd animals, such as sheep, goats, cattle, camels or llamas.

**Pillar stone:** a slab or block of stone often relating to stone circles, standing stones, or stone alignments.

**Pleistocene:** the geological epoch preceding the present inter-glacial Holocene era. In Europe, characterised by massive ice sheets covering large areas of the continent. Globally the Pleistocene spans the period between 1.8 million years ago to *c.* 10,000 years ago.

**Polished stone axe:** polished, or ground, stone tools are common in the Neolithic. Grinding coarse stone, which might be unsuitable for flint knapping, was a time intensive practice. Polishing tools often resulted in stronger implements, which were used extensively during the Late Stone Age for forest clearance and other heavy work.

**Portal dolmen:** (see dolmen)

**Promontory fort:** a fortified enclosure, usually of stone, built on raised land, which projects from a hillside or cliff. In Ireland, the best known example of a promontory fort is Dún Aenghus on Inis Mór in the Aran Islands.

**Radiocarbon dating:** a method of dating carbon-based material, by measuring the half-life of carbon 14; most effective on samples dating from 500 to 50,000 years ago.

**Rath/Ráith:** a circular earthen wall, often accompanied with additional fortifications in the form of palisades, surrounding a dwelling or dwellings. Can also be referred to as a ring fort.

**Recumbent stone:** a horizontally laid stone. In Ireland, stone circles typically have one or more recumbent stones associated with them.

**Ring barrow:** a burial characterised by a circular, raised earthen bank enclosing a (usually) single burial. Commonly associated with the Bronze Age, ring barrows were used until the Early Christian era in Ireland.

**Ring fort:** over 45,000 ring forts have been identified in Ireland. They are fortified settlements, which were used from the Iron Age through the Early Medieval period. Also known as rath/ráith, caiseal, cathair/caher, and dún. A rath is an earthen structure, caiseals and cahers are stone, and dún refers to a substantial, possibly elite structure such as Dún Ailinne in County Kildare.

**Ringed enclosure:** (see henge); also an earthen or stone enclosure, which defines a cemetery, or some other ritual or ceremonial area.

**Rock art:** any man-made markings on stone, including petroglyphs (stone carvings) and pictographs (rock and cave paintings). Nearly 30% of all known stone carvings in Europe are located in Ireland.

**Roof-box:** archaeologically, a purpose-built opening above a doorway, for the observation of a celestial event. Examples include those at Newgrange and Tomb G at Carrowkeel.

**Royal site:** in Ireland, royal sites are those associated with the five ancient provinces of Ireland: Mídhe (Hill of Tara), Leinster (Dún Ailinne), Ulster (Navan Fort/Emain Macha), Connaught (Rathcroghan), and Munster (Cashel).

**Shell midden:** also referred to as a kitchen midden; an archaeological feature made principally of mollusk shells, animal bones, and other household waste. Middens indicate areas of human habitation.

**Souterrain:** a narrow, elongated, subterranean passageway or gallery, usually of drystone, with a stone slab roof. In Ireland, souterrains can date to the Iron Age, but most commonly are found associated with the Early Christian through to medieval periods. Their exact function is the subject of discussion, but most likely souterrains were used for both cold storage and as places of refuge when under threat.

**Spindle whorl:** a small disc of stone or ceramic with a central hole, which is used when spinning wool. Spindle whorls act as fly-wheels to help maintain the rotation of the spindle as the fibres are separated from fleece.

**Standing stone:** a prehistoric monument consisting of a single, upright stone embedded in the earth. In Ireland, standing stones are commonly found in Late Neolithic and Bronze Age contexts.

**Stone alignment:** more than two standing stones arranged in a row.

**Táin bó Cúailgne:** (The Cattle Raid of Cooley). An epic story thought to have originated around the time of Christ, and written down by Christian monks during the eighth century. It concerns the war between Queen Medb of Connaught and King Conchobar MacNessa and the hero Cúchullain of Ulster, over the Brown Bull of Cooley. During the Iron Age, wealth was measured in cattle, and ownership of prime stock was paramount.

**Torc:** a metal neck ring, often of gold, and commonly associated with Bronze Age and Iron Age Ireland, and Europe.

**Triskele:** the triple spiral design found within the passageway of Newgrange.

**Túatha de Danann:** literally, the tribe or people of the god Danann or Anan. In Irish mythology, believed to be the supernatural predecessors of the first human inhabitants (the Milesians) in Ireland, who were later banished to the underworld. Oweynagat Cave in the Rathcroghan complex, County Roscommon, is often referred to as the entrance to the underworld.

**Urnfield culture:** a Late Bronze Age (1300-750 BCE), central European culture. Urnfielders earn their name from their custom of burying their cremated dead in urns in large, flat fields.

**Votive offering:** an object or group of objects, left in a sacred or ritual place for religious purposes.

**Wattle and daub:** a building material of woven rods or twigs, plastered with mud or clay.

**Wedge tomb:** a Late Neolithic through Early Bronze Age chamber tomb, constructed of large recumbent stones, and heavy capstones, in the shape of a large wedge. Most burials are cremations; though typically Bronze Age reuse of tombs includes inhumation burials.

# ONE

# DISCOVERING ANCIENT IRELAND

## THE IDEA OF 'PREHISTORY'

This is a book about Ireland, from the time the first peoples arrived around 9000 BCE, until the time when the first Christians came to settle and to convert the pagan tribes of the Iron Age. It is a book about 'prehistory', the period of time the modern world considers to be primitive and simple. Prehistory is anything but simple and primitive, however. To label it as such demonstrates a serious lack of understanding of the cultures who laid the framework of today's modern civilisations. In Ireland, it is a time that precedes writing as we recognise and understand it. It is a time of memory, symbols, and abstract cosmologies. In prehistoric times, the Irish established settlements; organised themselves in bands, tribes, and chiefdoms; developed belief systems; participated in vast trade networks; built great architectural monuments, many of which still stand; fought wars; held celebrations; loved their children; worshipped in special places; mined copper; hunted wild animals; established farms; mourned their dead; cleared forests; crafted beautiful ornaments of gold; and told stories of their lives that were so important to Irish culture, they have survived into the modern era.

As you read through the contents of this book, I will tend to use BCE (Before Common Era), rather than 'years ago', when writing of the prehistoric cultures of Ireland. This is a common archaeological usage. The year 0 (*Anno Domini*) denotes the change in archaeological dating from BCE to AD. Adding 2,000 years to a date which uses BCE, will give you an approximate date before the present day (e.g. 4000 BCE is the same as 6,000 years ago). This book provides a road map through Irish prehistory, and stops at some sites which get very few visitors, and a few that get thousands each year. Within it are photographs of the sites, as well as driving (and often walking) directions to each. Each of the sites mentioned – and the thousands which aren't – holds a special place in Ireland's long history, and every site in the country deserves respect and care when being visited. Many are on private land and are under the care of the people who often farm the surrounding landscape. Some are under state care and enjoy active professional conservation. It is imperative that the sites you visit are left as they were found. Removing even one small stone degrades and damages the sites, and leaving behind anything from sweet wrappers, to cigarette butts, to 'offerings', impacts the sites and landscapes in negative ways. Care must be taken when accessing any site; most are left to the elements, are unmown, have sheep or cattle on them, and can be dangerous. Many do not have signs directing you to respect them; in this instance I ask explicitly that you do so. Don't climb on tombs, don't leave your initials or name carved or written on them, don't dishonour the dead, and don't destroy Ireland's great past through your ignorance or carelessness.

## A NOTE ON THE 'AGES OF MANKIND'

The ages of mankind have been devised to generally coincide with changes or additions to material culture. A simplified way to examine prehistory is to use the three-age system, which divides human prehistory into the Stone Age, Bronze Age, and Iron Age. In Europe, these divisions have been further sub-divided into the Paleolithic, Mesolithic, Neolithic, Chalcolithic (lithic=stone), Early, Middle and Late Bronze Age, and Hallstatt and La Tene Iron Age. In turn, as archaeologists have learned more about each of these eras, they have been further sub-divided and refined for specific regions or zones (e.g. Dowris Phase, Wessex Period, and Unrfielder), which may have left a particular influence or 'stamp' that marks it as outstanding or highly recognisable in the archaeological record.

## A CAPSULE PREHISTORY OF IRELAND

Some 12 to 14,000 years ago, as the massive ice sheets of the Pleistocene receded, and the present warm, inter-glacial period of the Holocene began, the land masses of the earth changed dramatically. Water that had been locked in the frozen wastes was released, sea levels rose, and the continents separated and slowly became defined as the world we know today. The glaciers also changed the land surfaces of the northern hemisphere, as they scraped across the landscape. U-shaped valleys formed, esker ridges were squeezed up from the earth, drumlins (similar to frost heaves on roads) popped up, and great boulders, called glacial erratics, were deposited often thousands of miles from their source. Over two thirds of Ireland's land surface was covered with glacial ice when the warming trend began. It had been a barren and inhospitable place inhabited by large herd animals that lived their lives free of human contact. With the warming trend, these large mammals died out, and were replaced by herds of deer, sheep, and wild pig.

Around 9,000 years ago, after the Holocene had settled in, the first human groups landed on Ireland's shores. We believe the first peoples came from Scotland, and began their lives in the north of Ireland, in places like Mount Sandel in present day Coleraine. Over a very short period of time, more people arrived, and left behind traces of their lives on the Dingle peninsula, near the Blackwater, on Lambey Island, and in the midlands, along the shores of Lough Boora and Lough Derraveragh. For thousands of years, the band societies of the Mesolithic era camped in temporary shelters near fresh water sources, and followed herds of deer, fished, and collected berries, nuts, eggs, and shellfish as they went along. They were nomadic hunter-gatherers and never developed permanent villages, and did not participate in a farming economy.

Between 5,000 and 6,000 years ago, a new economic way of life came to Ireland, as agriculture was introduced in the Neolithic. Humans and their hominid ancestors, who had spent millions of years foraging and constantly moving, put down roots in the Neolithic, built permanent homesteads, and began to manipulate the landscape to suit their new lifestyle. The Neolithic is the final phase of the Stone Age in Europe, and is characterised by the use of pottery, farming and stock rearing, settled communities and farmsteads, and complex rituals related to the dead and the seasons. The Neolithic farmers of Ireland left behind field systems, hut circles, pottery, and massive burial tombs in the form of court tombs, dolmens, and passage graves, such as those at Newgrange, Carrowmore, Carrowkeel, and Loughcrew. They oriented many of the tombs toward solstices and equinoxes, and cremated and interred their honoured dead within them. Many of the tombs are covered with complex, abstract art that has been chipped into the massive stones. The people of the Neolithic enjoyed a warmer and drier climate than the one we know today in Ireland. They cleared much of the island of the dense deciduous forests that covered it; they grew wheat, barley, and oats; raised sheep, domesticated wild pigs, and imported cattle from Britain; they hunted deer and exploited the resources of the sea; and they formed clustered settlements, within territories marked by monuments to their dead.

Around 4,000 years ago (or 2000 BCE), the climate suddenly worsened when a volcanic eruption of enormous proportions in Iceland sent great plumes of ash into the atmosphere. This climate of colder temperatures and much wetter seasons coincided with an increase in bog formation and a massive cultural change as well. Between 2000 and 1800 BCE, a new technology was being introduced throughout Europe. The discovery and exploitation of copper ores began toward the end of the Neolithic, and is often referred to as the Chalcolithic, or Copper-Stone Age. Evidence of extensive copper mining has been found throughout southern Ireland, especially in Ross Island, County Kerry, and Mount Gabriel in Cork. Soon people learned to combine copper with tin to make bronze, a much harder, denser, and stronger material than copper. Tin sources are scant in Ireland, and the early Irish smiths had to import tin from the nearest resource in Cornwall. Bronze was used in the production of many items including sickles, knives, and other farm and household items. It was also used for personal decoration and, perhaps most importantly, for weapons. The myriad artefacts made of bronze became highly-valued symbols of power and wealth, which most people of the Bronze Age could only aspire to own.

During the Bronze Age in Ireland and throughout Europe, social status based on wealth and power emerged. Leadership was no longer based on merit and ability as it had been in the Neolithic; it was based upon a single powerful person or family, who controlled access to resources. The leader lived in a large well-defended house, usually apart from the rest of the tribe. The territory of the tribe expanded, and was marked with standing stones, stone circles, stone alignments, and barrows. The megalithic monuments of the Neolithic slowly fell into disuse, though some, like the Mound of Hostages at Tara, continued to be used for burial by the Bronze Age peoples of the area. War and battle increased and devastating wounds from bronze weapons and large, crushing, stone mauls become more noticeable in the archaeological record.

Between 600 and 500 BCE, the Iron Age, the final prehistoric era in Europe, began in Ireland, some time after it was established on the continent and Britain. It took some time before iron came into common use in Ireland. It is only during the first century BCE that the metal became widespread on the island. Unlike the rest of Europe, Ireland did not suffer from the overt influence of the Iron Age tribes, who moved across the continent bringing new economies, languages, and technologies with them. In Ireland, the Iron Age seems to have come about through trade and the exchange of ideas, rather than conquest. Thus, the Irish Iron Age did not travel along the same temporal trajectory as the rest of Europe, and did not develop the same recognisable characteristics either. The Iron Age in Ireland developed nearly independently of the rest of Europe, taking its own course through the final stages of prehistory. It was during the Iron Age, that the great epics of early Irish folklore took form, and that the great centres of power at Tara, Dún Ailinne, Crúachain, and Navan Fort (Emain Macha) were built. Unlike the rest of Europe, the Romans never landed on Ireland's shores. The Irish were fully aware of Rome's conquest of their neighbours, and were active trading partners with Romano-Britain, but the archaeological evidence suggests only a few Romans ever came to Ireland. As Rome fell in the fifth century, the chiefdoms of Ireland met newcomers, who brought with them a new religion, new centres of learning, and a new civilisation. It was an invasion the Irish could not avoid.

In AD 431, Palladius was sent to Ireland by Pope Celestine. He brought with him the message of the Church in Rome, but he found the Irish people to be less than receptive, and he quickly returned home. Soon after him in 432, a young, eager man with ties to Ireland arrived to preach and convert the pagans. St Patrick realised much greater success than Palladius, and found that by comparing the natural world with his spiritual one, he was able to reach a common understanding with the Irish. He established a church, gained followers, and began converting the Irish in a bloodless revolution. Patrick was joined by St Brigid, an Irish woman who embraced his teachings, and was followed by St Ciaran (who founded Clonmacnoise), St Brendan (the Voyager), St Columba (who founded churches at Derry, Kells, Durrow, and Iona), and St Kevin (who founded Glendalough), among countless others. The coming of Christianity to Ireland brought an end to prehistory there. The monasteries and centres of learning that were established there, thrived for hundreds of years. Many of the churches attributed to the early Christians, are still in use today. Along with a new religion, they also taught the Irish to read and write, and the monks themselves recorded many of the folk tales and epics the Irish had passed down through the generations by oral tradition. While the rest of Europe languished in the Dark Ages, Ireland was a vibrant, energetic centre of culture and learning.

The map overleaf shows many of the sites mentioned in the following text. I have tried to include both popular ancient sites, such as Newgrange and Tara,

and less well-known ones, like Ferriter's Cove and the Uragh Stone Circle. My suggestion when seeing these sites, is to plan ahead and take your time, so you can savour and appreciate their extraordinary beauty and ingenuity. You cannot see all the sites mentioned in the text in a day, or even a week. Chose a region, enjoy the landscape, and plan to return to see the rest in the future. Remember that for all the sites mentioned in this text, there are thousands more that are not, some of which are spectacular (such as the Bronze Age Mooghaun Fort, or The Hill of Uisneach). Directions are included in the text. As you venture out to explore these sites, ask locals where other sites may be, or purchase Ordnance Survey Discovery Series Maps, which are detailed maps that include ancient and historic sites. Respect the sites and the surrounding landscapes. Remember that most are on privately owned, actively farmed land. Carry out everything you carry in; dress appropriately (wellies, rain gear, torch, mobile phone); don't tease the animals; and don't destroy, manipulate, climb on, or litter these fragile and important heritage sites.

All the photographs included herein, were taken by the author over the course of many years, with the exception of the photographs of the interior of Oweynagat Cave, which are used with the kind permission of Jessica Guertin.

TWO

# PALEOLITHIC AND MESOLITHIC (700000-4000 BCE)

In cultural-evolutionary terms, hominid history began in the Paleolithic (paleo=old/ancient; lithic=stone), roughly 5 million years ago. This time horizon is continually shifting backward, as more discoveries of truly ancient hominid remains are found. Hominids are bipedal primates, and include all species within the family of man, including modern humans as well our evolutionary ancestors. In Europe, the Paleolithic stretched from approximately 700,000 – 12,000 years before present, but in Ireland, there is no evidence of Paleolithic habitation. There are a number of reasons for this: the most recent European Ice Age, which only ended around 10-12,000 years ago, made the landscape inhospitable, and, as the ice sheets receded, the land mass of Ireland became isolated from the rest of Europe as sea levels rose. The Paleolithic people in southern Britain, where the ice sheets were less intrusive, do not seem to have ventured across the glacial landmass which led to Ireland.

The late or upper Paleolithic is considered to have lasted from about 40,000 – 12,000 years before present, or from the time of the last of the Neanderthals until the beginning of the Mesolithic, or Middle Stone Age. In geological terms, this is known as the Pleistocene-Holocene horizon. The withdrawal of the ice sheets at the end of the Pleistocene, marks the beginning of the geological epoch we are currently in, the Holocene. It is during the upper Paleolithic, that the rough toolkits of previous ages are replaced by intricate and well-crafted, stone tools, population begins to expand, forms of spiritual belief become evident in the archaeological record (such as the Venuses of central Europe), and artistic endeavours illustrating both abstract concepts and realistic domains become part of human life (an example would be the cave paintings at Las Caux).

Paleolithic sites have been found throughout much of Europe. Sites are usually identified by the stone tools and stone debris (called debitage) left behind as a result of making the tools. Paleolithic tools are distinctive, in that they are large, and would likely have not been hafted, such as the Acheulean Hand Axe. Along with an array of distinctive (or diagnostic) tools, sites often have the remains of animals hunted by Paleolithic groups. The small, kin-related groups were not settled at this time, but had a nomadic lifestyle called hunting and gathering. They generally hunted mega-fauna such as mammoth, aurochs (a species of very large ox), horse, and giant deer. They also would have exploited water fowl, fish, and shellfish, and were highly dependent on the movement of these large herd animals. Sites that indicate short-term habitation, are usually found near fresh water sources, and many in the Paleolithic are also found associated with caves.

## MESOLITHIC

The Mesolithic (meso=middle) begins at the end of the last Ice Age (or inter-glacial), around 12,000 years ago, and comes to an end when agriculture begins in the Neolithic, around 5,000 years ago. Mesolithic people still participated in hunting and gathering, but the stone toolkit changed quite dramatically from that of the people who came before them. Unlike the large, hand-held tools of the Paleolithic, early Mesolithic tools are much smaller, sharper, and are of a much wider variety. Diagnostic tools include, microliths (very small pieces of stone fashioned into tools), chipped and polished stone axes, and a wide array of blades. Tool makers, known as flint-knappers, would knock flakes of stone from a larger core, with a piece of antler or other 'hammer', or would 'stamp' or chisel long flakes from a core, using a method called 'direct percussion'.

### Hunter-gatherers or foragers

For more than 90% of hominid existence, hunting and gathering has been the primary cultural and economic activity of the earth's populations. In Mesolithic Ireland, hunter-gatherers, or foragers, although nomadic, were not constantly on the move. Rather, their lives revolved around the movement of the animals they hunted, and the resources they needed in order to survive. As the ice sheets of the Pleistocene receded, the large, herd animals, or mega-fauna, so common in the Paleolithic, such as mammoth and giant bison, likewise withdrew, and eventually became extinct as the climate warmed. In the warmer climate, Mesolithic groups had to learn to hunt different animals, and to fashion their lives on a much more seasonal basis. Ireland's Mesolithic peoples hunted deer, wild pig, and other mast feeders, and also depended on both fresh and salt water resources. They would have hunted fur-bearing animals, and the archaeological evidence shows they had a significant reliance on hazel nuts. The archaeological record indicates they enjoyed warmer, drier weather than we have now, and they also enjoyed resource-rich surroundings.

*Kin groups and band society*
Mesolithic people lived in small kin groups, and would have followed an egalitarian political system; leadership roles would have been fluid, based upon merit and ability. An egalitarian society does not mean everyone was equal, but it is believed they had a horizontal social organization, with little evidence of 'ranking' or clear social hierarchies. In most cases, evidence of social hierarchies in ancient cultures is found in burial practices and grave goods. Other European Mesolithic sites suggest that some groups may have had a system of ranking, but we do not find clear evidence of this in Ireland, because burials from the period have not been recovered. The kin groups would have been further organised into bands, which are the simplest form of human social organization. Bands consist of thirty to fifty people, all of whom are related through blood, marriage, adoption, or some other form of familial inclusion. Along with the egalitarian political system mentioned above, studies done on contemporary band societies have found most make decisions by consensus; have very informal leadership, again, based on merit, ability, wisdom, or age; possess no written laws or rules; have no police, or other coercive roles such as those in more complex societies; pass their traditions and customs on orally; and religious beliefs may be based on family tradition or transmitted through a shaman. A formalised system of social institutions would not exist in band society.

## MESOLITHIC LIFEWAYS

Mesolithic people all over Europe were at the mercy of the environment, and would have needed to make decisions quickly. With the change in climate at the beginning of the Holocene, and the accompanying changes in resources,

Mesolithic people were pressed to develop increasingly complex and specialised toolkits based on their local environment and resources. The large hand axes of the Paleolithic, used to butcher the mega-fauna of the era, were relatively useless on the smaller herd animals of the Mesolithic. Stone knives, microliths, specialized arrows and points, axes, and other tools were created and refined based on need and quarry. We don't know how Mesolithic peoples treated their dead in Ireland as no burials have yet been found. Evidence from other areas of Europe suggests later Mesolithic people did have a formalised system related to death and burial. It is likely, late Mesolithic groups in Ireland developed small cemeteries like their continental neighbours, but their location on coastal areas, near inland waterways, or in marshes, has made their identification and recovery difficult.

War and conflict would have been comparatively rare during the Mesolithic, but there is some clear evidence in other areas of Europe that conflict did occur and was quite brutal. At Ofnet Cave in Bavaria, a pit containing thirty-eight decapitated skulls was recovered, which dates to 8500 BCE, about the time of Ireland's first known period of human habitation (Thorpe, 2000). Most were women and children under the age of fifteen. The skulls in the pit were covered with red ochre, a common colouring used in burial during the Mesolithic, and were accompanied by an array of animal bones and teeth. Cave burial would have been common in the Mesolithic, but, as stated above, thus far, no burials dating from the Mesolithic period have been recovered in Ireland. This is likely to be due to acidic soil conditions, or possibly to the method Mesolithic bands in Ireland used to dispose of their dead.

## EARLY MESOLITHIC IN IRELAND (7000-5500 BCE)

*Mount Sandel, Coleraine, County Derry*
In Ireland, the earliest known habitation took place in the early Mesolithic, after the ice sheets had withdrawn. One of the earliest known Mesolithic sites is Mount Sandel near Coleraine in County Derry, Northern Ireland. This important site, on a hilltop overlooking the River Bann, was excavated in the 1970s by Peter Woodman, who found some of earliest recorded structural remains in Ireland (Mallory and McNeill 1991). Woodman found evidence of several huts, indicated by a series of post- or stake-holes, circling an interior

hearth. Radiocarbon dates indicate the site was occupied in around 7000 BCE. Though we don't know for sure how the huts were made, or what they were covered with, archaeologists surmise that the narrow poles, or saplings, were lashed together at the top, and then covered with hides, bark, or turf. These would not have been permanent dwellings, and would likely only have been used seasonally, as the people who built them took part in their seasonal migrations. Hazelnut remains found at Mount Sandel indicate the site was occupied in the autumn and early winter; faunal remains such as pig, salmon and eel suggest the site was also used in late winter, spring, and summer for short periods of time (Mallory and McNeill, 1991). Clearly the area was rich in resources, and was very attractive to the people who stopped there for generations, during the early Mesolithic in Ireland. The site appears to have been abandoned in around 6000 BCE.

The Mesolithic site at Mount Sandel is no longer visible, but the large Iron Age fort, from which the site takes its name, is. To reach the site it is best to take the path beginning at the Coleraine Court House on Mount Sandel Road.

*Lough Boora, County Offaly*
Lough Boora, in County Offaly, is another early Mesolithic site roughly contemporary with Mount Sandel. Also known as Boora Beg, this site was occupied between 7,000 and 6,800 BCE. Hundreds of stone blades and microliths were found, as well as polished, stone axes. A majority of the stone tools recovered were made from black chert, a type of flint which holds a sharp edge, and is relatively easy to work. Many of the tools found at Lough Boora, such as the polished axes, suggest hafting to wood, bone, or antler handles (Waddell, 2000). The site is located near the village of Kilcormac, and has been incorporated into a Mesolithic Walk, within the Lough Boora Parklands. Lough Boora was a lakeshore settlement, which has since been covered by bog. The diet included local trout, eel, wild pig, wood pigeon, and hazelnuts.

What is especially important about Lough Boora is that until its excavation, it was assumed that early settlers to Ireland would only be found near the shoreline areas, such as at Mount Sandel. The site of Lough Boora demonstrates that human groups dispersed throughout the island, including the resource-rich midlands. Since its discovery in the 1970s, other inland sites such as Lough Derraveragh described below, support the notion that Mesolithic people were eager to take advantage of a wide array of resources across Ireland.

Lough Boora, County Offaly. The Mesolithic site once located here is no longer visible.

To reach the Lough Boora Parklands, travel along the N52, from either Tullamore to the north, or Birr from the south, to the R357. The Lough Boora Parklands are very, well sign-posted. The best approach to the site is along the 'sculpture trail', which begins at the small car park, across from the thatched bird hide. The trail is well marked, but is quite long, at nearly 2km, and can be buggy if the weather is humid. The Mesolithic site is no longer visible, but the landscape of the Lough will give visitors a clear impression of the conditions Mesolithic people faced in the Midlands 9,000 years ago.

## THE LATER MESOLITHIC (5500-2500 BCE)

Beginning in around 5500 BCE, there was a change in the tool production techniques of Mesolithic peoples in Ireland. John Waddell has pointed out, that the flint knapping of the early Mesolithic, was replaced by 'direct percussion' production, which resulted in heavier, more robust blades (2000:16). By the late Mesolithic, the population in Ireland had grown, though was still relatively sparse. People were exploring and exploiting more areas of the island, and evidence of their hunting, gathering, and living spaces become more common in the archaeological record. Diagnostic tools of this period include the distinctive 'Bann Flake', a leaf-shaped, stone blade, first identified from sites along the River Bann, in Northern Ireland. Microliths, and small projectile points seem to have gone out of fashion in the later Mesolithic. Waddell suggests Bann Flakes may have been multi-purpose tools, used for cutting, scraping, wood-working, and possibly as spear heads. Not every tool would have been made of stone; it is likely wooden spears, bone harpoons and points, and netting of grass and bark were also used, but these parts of the Mesolithic toolkit simply have not survived in great quantity into the present day. Some exceptions, such as bits of worked wood and bone from a few sites, suggest Mesolithic people were adept at utilising a wide variety of materials. Dug-out canoes (such as the Lurgan boat in the National Museum, Kildare Street, Dublin), indicate how important the exploitation of water resources was for many people during the Irish Mesolithic.

*Ferriter's Cove, Dingle Peninsula, County Kerry*
Ferriter's Cove, at the western end of the Dingle peninsula, shows evidence of a Mesolithic campsite that had been used over and over again for several hundred years. The site was excavated by Peter Woodman, in the 1980s, after a Neolithic plano-convex, flint blade was discovered nearby. What Woodman found was unexpected. Several lenses of shells were discovered in a series of shell middens, all of which contained Mesolithic artefacts, including hundreds of blades, burins, punches, polished stone axes, and flakes. The shell middens indicate the people of Ferriter's Cove were very dependent upon the resources easily accessed within the sheltered cove. Radiocarbon dates on the shell, bone, and other remains, suggest the area was used as a temporary camp over the course of several hundred years, from about 5600 BCE (or about 7,600 years ago) (Harbison 1988; O'Kelly 1989). Wild pig, deer, and fish were also recovered, from what Michael O'Kelly called, the 'living or squatting areas', which demonstrates that Mesolithic visitors to Ferriter's Cove had adapted to their immediate environment, and also had a wide variety of protein resources available to them (1989: 29).

To reach the picturesque area of Ferriter's Cove, begin at the town of Dingle, and proceed along the Slea Head Road. Ferriter's Cove is located in the hamlet of Ballyferriter.

Ferriter's Cove, Dingle Peninsula, County Kerry. It is in this small cove that a number of Mesolithic artefacts were found protruding from the banks.

Lough Derravaragh, Mullingar, County Westmeath. Lough Derravaragh is steeped in myth being associated with the story of the Children of Lir. It is also the site of a number of the earliest Mesolithic sites in Ireland.

*Lough Derraveragh, Mullingar, County Westmeath*

Other sites of the later Mesolithic include, Lough Derraveragh in County Westmeath north of Mullingar, Sutton, near Howth, on the north of Dublin Bay, and Dalkey Island, on south Dublin Bay. As the Mesolithic drew to a close, many sites began to show signs of an 'overlap' with the Neolithic, or New Stone Age period which follows. Dalkey Island contains a large Mesolithic shell midden, the upper layers of which contain bits of Neolithic pottery, and the bones of domesticated animals (O'Kelly, 1989; Waddell, 2000). Likewise the site of Sutton, to the north, and the middens at Rockmarshall, in County Louth indicate people at various stages of transition were utilising the sites; along with a variety of later Mesolithic tools, and radiocarbon (C14) dates, which suggest the later Mesolithic, Neolithic materials, and fauna have also been recovered (Harbison, 1988; O'Kelly, 1989; Waddell, 2000). This blurred transition from one cultural period to another, is typical throughout history. Farming, which is the socio-economic watershed of the Neolithic, would have been a significantly different way of life for nomadic people to adapt to. It is likely that the development of farming and a settled lifestyle, where one is tied to the land would have been a slow shift away from the foraging life enjoyed by Mesolithic peoples in Ireland. The archaeological evidence from the later Mesolithic suggests that many groups in Ireland clung to hunting and gathering for up to a thousand years after farming began. In many cases, this may be due to what Marshall Sahlins (1971) called, 'the original affluent society'; despite what modern cultures may view as a difficult, and highly unpredictable way of life, hunter-gatherers generally enjoyed rather easy and relaxed lives, interspersed with periods of movement and industry.

Why, and how, did Mesolithic people in Ireland begin to practice farming? Even though Ireland can be seen as an isolated territory because it is an island, it is known that people travelled, at the very least, to Britain, by boat. Farming was well established in the south of Britain during the later Mesolithic in Ireland, and travellers from Ireland, would have observed the practice, and may have traded for a variety of agricultural products and goods on their travels. It is also assumed, that people from abroad came to Ireland, bringing their knowledge and industries with them. These exchanges and migrations would influence the Stone Age cultures on either side of the sea. By roughly 6,000 years ago in Ireland, the Mesolithic way of life had given way to Neolithic farmers, and settled communities.

THREE

# THE NEOLITHIC (4000-2000 BCE)

Six thousand years ago, the transition from a hunter-gatherer lifestyle, to an agricultural one, began to spread across Ireland. The Neolithic, the final phase of the Stone Age in Europe, is recognised through a number of cultural changes and inventions: agriculture, settled communities and farmsteads, pottery, social hierarchies, bounded territories, and megalithic monuments. It was a time of extraordinary change and creativity.

## AGRICULTURE

The domestication of plants and animals necessitated settlement, but these did not occur all at once. Over the course of time, people throughout Europe would have begun to practice horticulture (the cultivation of garden plants), and also would have begun raising young animals, perhaps the offspring of adult animals they had hunted. Through trade and other contacts, the practice of agriculture and animal husbandry began to diffuse across the continent. As people began to depend more and more on their gardens and livestock, they also began to build permanent settlements to accommodate them. Their lives began to revolve around their locality, rather than the seasonal migrations of the animals they had previously hunted.

   In Ireland, people domesticated sheep, goats, pigs, and cattle, as well as cats and dogs. Cattle, sheep, and goats are not native to Ireland, and were probably introduced from Scotland. Harbison suggests, based upon faunal remains from the Sutton (County Dublin) Mesolithic midden, that either Irish Late

Mesolithic people, or Neolithic intruders, brought cattle to Ireland during the transition period (1988). Pollen remains, and carbonised plant materials, indicate people in Europe were planting wheat (einkorn and emmer) and barley among other early domesticates.

## POTTERY

Necessity is the mother of invention, and the beginning of agriculture necessitated the creation of a variety of containers, for the surplus foods the Neolithic farmers were harvesting. A simple element of our household, which modern peoples take for granted, pottery, was highly valued during the Stone Age. Usually made from local clays, tempered with local materials, the earliest pots were used for storing and cooking the wheat, barley, and other grains harvested in the early autumn. Any surplus products would have been stored in pits, often within the house, and the inhabitants would extract what they needed over the course of the year. As Neolithic people refined their pottery making, the repertoire of designs became more specialised and varied.

Five thousand years ago, pottery was made using a paddle and coil method (the pottery wheel was a much later invention). The clay would be rolled out into long strips, and then coiled and pressed into the form needed. It would then be paddled smooth, and fired in an open fire. The result was not pottery or ceramics as we recognise today, but a rough, unglazed, thick, and unrefined container.

## SETTLED COMMUNITIES

With agriculture comes forest clearance, and within a short span of time, the Neolithic farming communities of Ireland had cleared large areas of forest using a combination of slash and burn, 'ringing', and felling techniques. Ringing is a technique whereby large strips of bark are removed in rings, around a tree trunk, resulting in the death of the tree. Homesteads and farmsteads, rather than villages, would have been the norm in the early Neolithic, and these would have been based upon the family unit. As time went on, small villages, sometimes within earthen-walled, or bank and ditch, enclosures, grew up around the island.

Homes were constructed of a variety of materials, including stone, earth, wood, and wattle and daub. The remains of all such structures have been found in the archaeological record. It is assumed, the family unit during the Neolithic was the extended family, but this assumption is based upon modern-day cultures, which follow a similar lifestyle. House-size seems to have been dictated by both the number of people who lived there, and the status of the family; the larger and more elaborate the house, the higher the status of the people within it.

House-styles could be round, elliptical, square, or rectangular. It is likely the roofs were thatch, or covered with turf, or sheets of bark. There would have been a central hearth, which was a source of heat, as well as a cooking area. Much of what we have learned about Neolithic family life, we have learned from excavating hearths. Remains of meals, pottery, personal items, and broken weapons and flake debitage, among other artefacts, have been found in and around the cooking fires of Neolithic homes. Because much of the organic material has been carbonised, they have also provided archaeologists with dating materials. Studies at the Neolithic settlement of Skara Brae, in Scotland, suggest the interiors would have been divided into male and female spaces, and likely also would have included children's and elders' spaces, based on the sizes of the stone bed frames and types of artefacts recovered. Again, the size of the dwelling, would likely have depended upon the size and status of the family who occupied it.

## SOCIAL HIERARCHIES

With settled communities, came the beginnings of social hierarchies. During the Neolithic, social organisation moved from the egalitarianism evident in the Mesolithic, to one where social ranking becomes increasingly important. This is linked to the tribalism of Neolithic peoples, as well as the notion of territory. Tribal territory would need to be defended from outsiders, and those who could demonstrate the ability to lead in times of conflict, may have been held in high esteem. Belief systems would have also been important in establishing tribal leaders; those who could interpret the natural and supernatural worlds of the tribe, would also have been seen as leaders. It is not known if these positions were exclusive to men. Elaborate burial chambers contained the burnt remains of both men and women, and both could be entombed with a wealth of grave goods, which indicate status. Tribal members who possessed particular skills, such as a potter, flint-knapper, or tool-maker, would also have held rank within the community. There also would have been lower-class labourers, and probably slaves, captured from conflicts with territorial raiders.

## BOUNDED TERRITORIES

As kin groups and bands began to settle down, it became necessary for them to identify territories that were bounded. Unlike the nomadic bands of the Mesolithic, where territory was fluid and malleable, Neolithic farmers had specific areas that were personal, familial, and tribal. Personal space would have included the homestead and its contents, the kitchen garden, and perhaps small enclosures close to the house, for animals. Familial, or kin space, might range further, to include the crops and pastures cleared and planted by the kin group. Tribal space would be wide-ranging, covering vast territories, often marked by ritual areas such as stone circles, standing stones, or burial tombs.

It is in the Neolithic, that we begin to see defensive structures around both homesteads and the tribal centres of power. Often these would be simple bank and ditch structures, or palisades built in such a way as to keep the approaching group both visible and single file. Ditches could also be structured to disable those who would try to attack, by being so narrow at the bottom, and so steep that they could snap an enemy's ankles. Weapons, and injuries from conflict, become more common in association with the skeletal remains of Neolithic peoples, a further indication of the need to either defend or attack territories.

## MEGALITHS

Among the most recognisable structures of the Neolithic, are the megalithic monuments that are found in a variety of forms across the continent of Europe. Perhaps the best known European monument is Stonehenge, on Salisbury Plain in England, which was built and rebuilt over a span of 1,500 years, from about 3500 BC. In Ireland, megalithic monuments are generally related to burial places, whether people are buried within them or not. Newgrange, located in the Boyne Valley, of County Meath, is the most famous of Ireland's megalithic burial monuments.

Megaliths, as stated above, are generally associated with burials. In the Neolithic, the people placed inside the burial chambers, would have been cremated outside the tombs, after going through a period of de-fleshing. It is thought that the bodies of those privileged enough to be placed in a burial tomb would first be laid out in the elements over several weeks or months, in order for the soft tissue to decay or be stripped away by animals. The de-fleshing process made it easier and more efficient to cremate the remains prior to placing them within a tomb. Most tombs would be used for several generations, before being closed or abandoned.

Not everyone would be interred in a burial monument; the number of individuals identified within them is only a small percentage of the actual number of people who would have lived in Europe during the Neolithic. Because of this, it is thought that an elite class had emerged, who could enjoy the benefits of special treatment in preparation for the afterlife. Many of the monuments in Europe (and certainly in Ireland), are also adorned with complex artwork, which has been pecked into the large stones with hammer stones. We will never know what the symbols mean, but many of the designs seem to represent waterways, celestial bodies, plants, and landscapes. The abstract symbols illustrate the lives and beliefs of the peoples of the Neolithic.

There are a large variety of Neolithic burial tombs evident in Ireland. These include passage tombs, wedge tombs, portal dolmens, and court tombs. Passage tombs, such as Newgrange, were constructed from about 3500 BCE, and many were used over and over again until the early centuries AD. Court tombs, such as Creevykeel, seem to have coincided with the development of the larger passage tombs. Portal dolmens, like Poulnabrone and Proleek, and those at Carrowmore, were first seen on the landscape, from about 2500 to 2000 BCE, and wedge tombs seem to be the final manifestation of megalithic burial chamber in Ireland, which appear between 2000 and 1500 BCE.

In addition to megalithic monuments, Neolithic people began a tradition of constructing huge earthen enclosures, which carried on into the Iron Age and the Early Christian period.


## SUMMARY

As the nomadic, egalitarian, band society of the Mesolithic came to an end, a settled, highly-organised, agricultural way of life began to take hold across

Europe. Kin groups settled in tribal territories, and cleared forest lands, in order to plant crops and rear newly-domesticated sheep, cattle, goats, and pigs. They built houses and farmsteads, with kitchen gardens, close to their tilled fields and pastures. Pottery and farming tools were developed, as well as social networks based on trade and exchange. Conflict between and among tribal groups, though not common, becomes more evident in the archaeological record of the Neolithic. Social organization is much more complex than in the Mesolithic; social hierarchies develop, and social elites emerge. These social elites are often cremated and buried within the large megalithic monuments, which appear to stand as markers of tribal territories, frequently located on high ground or in wide, open spaces, visible for many miles. These monuments, used for several generations, are highly-decorated with complex, abstract rock carvings, the meanings of which we may never know.

## THE NEOLITHIC TIMELINE IN IRELAND

The first Neolithic peoples in Ireland would have been making the transition from the nomadism of their predecessors, to the fully settled life of agriculturalists. Over the course of a period, from roughly 4000 to 3500 BCE, these first Neolithic communities probably followed a pastoral lifestyle, herding domesticated animals seasonally, to adequate pastures. Much like Mesolithic people, they would have lived in temporary housing, or camps, depending on where their animals were grazing. At this time, cereal cultivation would have been less important than stock raising, and there would have been less dramatic evidence of forest clearance. Early Neolithic folk would have created rough pottery for the storage and cooking of grains, though pottery became more common as they became more settled. Once the tradition of kitchen gardening and cereal cultivation took hold, during the fourth millennium BCE, settled farmsteads become more evident in the archaeological record. This period, generally referred to as the Middle Neolithic, is most apparent in the development of decorated pottery, settled farmsteads and cereal cultivation, as well as pasturage and livestock enclosures. Palynology, the study of pollen, gives us a virtual landscape of prehistory, and archaeologists have determined the degree of forest clearances, and the types of cereals planted throughout time. These changes took place across Ireland, and within a few centuries, cultivation and stock-raising and the clearing of land was the dominant lifestyle.

The Legannany Dolmen, near Ballynahinch, County Down.

The landscape of the Brú na Bóinne with Newgrange in the distance. This photograph was taken from the southern bank of the River Boyne, County Meath.

The late Neolithic peoples were making a transition from the final stages of the Stone Age, to the introduction of metals in the Bronze Age in around 2000-1800 BCE. They had a highly-developed agricultural industry, a social organization based on tribal territories, and an advanced funerary culture concentrated upon great megalithic burial structures. Pottery styles had refined and changed from the round bottomed 'Beaker' pottery of the past, to large, flat-bottomed containers covered in decoration, such as those found during excavations at Newgrange, in the Boyne Valley. Trade with Britain, and places further afield, became more common, as evidenced by a variety of trade goods found throughout Ireland. People were also spinning wool from their sheep (which were quite hairy, rather than woolly); archaeologists have found round spindle whorls, impressions of rough cloth in clay, and waterlogged bits of material in bogs.

Newgrange from the western side, showing the magnificent surrounding kerb stones, part of the stone circle, and the quartz and granite facing of the mound.

The entrance stone at Newgrange. Behind the deeply-carved stone can be seen the entrance to the passage tomb and the 'roof box', which the winter solstice sunrise shines down each year to illuminate the passage. The dark grey stones are not original to the structure, but were installed to recess the passage, so the entrance stone could be preserved.

## NEOLITHIC SITES IN IRELAND

There are countless sites in Ireland, which date from the Neolithic, so only a few will be outlined here. Some of them are well-preserved and popular sites to visit, but most of the ones mentioned here are off the beaten path, although highly representative of the extraordinary creativity and expressiveness of the period. Few sites have visible remains of house structures, many show evidence of field systems in use prior to the increase in bog growth, around 2700 BCE, but many still retain the remains of ceremonial places and burial tombs. As with the sites throughout this book, driving/hiking directions to each site are given. And, as with any site of archaeological and historical importance, it is vital to respect and care for them.

*Newgrange, Knowth, Dowth, and the Brú na Boínne*
Any exploration of Neolithic Ireland would begin at the most well-known site grouping, at the Bend of the Boyne River, in County Meath, north of Dublin. Newgrange, Knowth and Dowth are part of the Boyne Valley, or Brú na Boínne World Heritage Site. Newgrange, Knowth and Dowth were all constructed more than 5,000 years ago, to house the dead of the people who lived nearby. They are three very large, and very conspicuously-located passage tombs. Prior to re-forestation in the historic period, the tombs would have been visible from each other, as well as from several other smaller tumuli and vantage points across the Boyne Valley.

Newgrange is a large 'cruciform' passage tomb (seventy-six meters in diameter), which contained cremation burials in all three of its chambers. First investigated by the antiquarian, Edward Llwyd, in 1699, the tomb wasn't scientifically excavated, until Professor Michael O'Kelly's work in the 1960s and 1970s. At the same time, Dr George Eogan began work at Knowth. Dowth, the least well known and examined of the three main tombs, is believed to have collapsed some centuries ago, and was further damaged by unscientific investigation in the mid-nineteenth century. These excavations contributed to the noticeable deterioration of the tomb's condition, and today, it resembles the mouth of a volcano. Dowth may be the most ancient of the large passage tombs here, and measures ninety meters in diameter, and is about fifteen meters in height. Two passages on the western side of the tomb are still visible, though one is a much later (and shorter) souterrain. The main passage is partially collapsed, but can still be explored (with permission), by using a later souterrain entrance which links to it.

The stone circle at Newgrange. Erected some time after the passage tomb was completed, only a few of the original stones of the circle remain.

Front view of Newgrange.

The standing stone to the south of Newgrange, located just inside the modern enclosure. The spiral carving at the bottom is a symbol that is repeated at many sites in Ireland.

O'Kelly's meticulous excavations at Newgrange were the culmination of an illustrious career at University College Cork. What he found was extraordinary and unexpected. As excavations progressed, he found ninety-seven kerb stones, which had been covered by the mound as it gradually slumped away over the millennia. They were richly-decorated with intricate rock art. The orthostats and many of the lintels in the eighteen-meter long interior passage, were also covered with carved chevrons, spirals, swirls, and cup and ring marks. More curiously, he found that many of the stones, were also decorated on the sides and edges that would not have been visible when the tomb was in use. The cruciform chamber (a large central area with three smaller chambers in the shape of a cross), was also decorated, the centre chamber was adorned with the now famous triple spiral, or triskele, design. O'Kelly also found an unusual 'roof-box' at the entrance to the long, narrow passage. It was later discovered that at sunrise, on the winter solstice, the sun's rays would shine through the roof-box, gradually moving along the passage, until it lit upon the central orthostat with the triskele design (O'Kelly, 1972). Newgrange is not limited to the large passage tomb but also retains remnants of a large Bronze-Age stone circle (though many of the upright stones have disappeared), smaller related tombs, and footprints of Neolithic huts. Across the vista can also be seen several other passage tombs among the fields still actively farmed.

O'Kelly's interpretation of the passage tomb was met with some controversy in the archaeological community. The quartz stones, and water-rolled boulders that were found encircling the mound, as the excavations reached the Neolithic ground level, were a puzzling anomaly. Neither are local to the Boyne Valley (the quartz came from Wicklow to the south, and the granite water-rolled boulders from Dundalk Bay to the north). O'Kelly reconstructed a rather fantastic façade for the tomb, which only adds to its grandeur. Many archaeologists have criticized his awe-inspiring reconstruction, suggesting a less impressive interpretation. Nonetheless, today the Newgrange visitor can avail of a spectacular site, which is a testament to the complexities of perception of Ireland's Neolithic ancestors.

George Eogan, of University College Dublin, undertook excavations at Knowth, about the same time O'Kelly was excavating Newgrange. Eogan was able to conduct his excavations without the spotlight O'Kelly endured for much of his work. Because of this, he had the luxury of stretching his excavations over nearly forty years. Work at Knowth continues even today. Professor Eogan (now retired from University College Dublin), has written several volumes on his excavations at Knowth, and still participates in the research of the site. He also excavated the passage tomb at Fourknocks, and worked on the excavations at the Mound of Hostages, at the Hill of Tara. When he first began his research at Knowth, the site as we know it today could never have been imagined. A large 80 by 90m passage tomb with two long passages (each over thirty meters in length), one running east and one west, and decorated with over one third of all the known megalithic rock art in Western Europe, Knowth also has eighteen existing smaller satellite tombs, none of which were visible when Eogan started his excavations. As these emerged, it became obvious that Eogan was unearthing one of the most unique and spectacular passage tomb cemeteries in the world (Herity and Eogan 1977; Malone, C. 2001; Stout 2002).

The River Boyne from Knowth.

Knowth is positioned west of Newgrange, on a ridge which overlooks the Boyne River. Its satellite tombs, though much smaller than the central one, have all their entrances pointing toward the main tomb. Over 300 of the interior orthostats, and external kerb stones at Knowth, are decorated with megalithic art, some of which are as perplexing as they are spectacular. We will never know with any certainty exactly what the symbols on the stones mean, but many scholars and others have speculated as to some of their meanings. One stone seems to resemble a sundial, others seem to reflect the winding nature of the river, and others the cosmos. Along with its incredible rock art, many unique and beautiful artefacts were recovered during excavation, including a striking engraved stone mace head, stone urns, carved basin stones, Carrowkeel ware pottery, and glass and bone beads. Many of these are currently on permanent display at the National Museum, on Kildare Street, in Dublin, and replicas of some are located in the Brú na Boínne Visitor's Centre.

The central passage tomb at Knowth with satellite tombs. As Knowth was excavated by George Eogan, eighteen small satellite tombs were discovered, which had been completely obscured by thousands of years of soil accumulation.

The central passage tomb at Knowth with satellite tombs.

The central passage tomb at Knowth with satellite tombs.

*Above:* A satellite tomb at Knowth showing the entrance, kerb stones, and passage.

*Left:* The west entrance at Knowth with standing stone, boulder, and heavily-carved entrance stone. Note that Eogan interpreted the quartz and granite differently than O'Kelly did at Newgrange. Eogan undertsood the quartz and granite as a frontier between the sacred and mundane, choosing to leave the stones on the ground at the entrances.

*This page and overleaf:* Carved kerb stones at Knowth. Nearly every kerb stone at Knowth is carved with abstract designs, the meaning of which is lost to us.

The 'sundial' stone at Knowth.

Unlike O'Kelly's interpretation of the great quartz and granite walls facing Newgrange, Eogan felt the quartz and water-rolled granite had been used as paving stones near the two entrances of the great tomb at Knowth. His interpretation seems to suggest a separation between the lived worlds outside of the tomb, and the underworld, or world of the dead, within the tomb. People would have had to pass over and through the paving stones in order to be admitted to the interior passages. Even today, when visitors enter the tombs, they must pass over the line, which divides the two worlds. Eogan also found evidence of a 'woodhenge' near the entrance to the main tomb, which may have been used as a ceremonial space by the people who came to Knowth.

Knowth was not only used during the Neolithic, but shows evidence of consistent use in the Iron Age, until well into the Norman period. Very little activity at Knowth seems to have taken place during the Bronze Age, and there has been speculation that the place may have been seen as untouchable, or of such sacred value to the past, that it should not be disturbed. One Beaker burial of a cremation with a Beaker pot in a pit was recovered, and it stands as the only confirmed Beaker burial to date in Ireland. Eogan recovered evidence of a palisaded-structure, built atop the great mound, that was later enlarged into a fortified-house during the Norman period. The site may also have been exploited by the early Christians, and others, who saw its location as a good vantage point.

Woodhenge at Knowth, a large, wooden circle located near the eastern entrance. It is thought people would gather within the wooden circle, for ceremonies and rituals related to the activities at Knowth.

The very degraded Dowth monument, the third great passage tomb of the Brú na Bóinne.

The sites of Newgrange and Knowth are only accessible through the Brú na Bóinne Centre, adjacent to the tombs. Knowth is not accessible during the winter months, and both tombs often have queues. Photographs are allowed at Knowth, both in the interior and exterior, while at Newgrange photographs are not allowed inside the passage tomb. The Brú na Bóinne Centre is located in County Meath, north of Dublin. It can be reached from the N2, and is well sign-posted from the motorway.

*Knocknarea, Carrowmore Megalithic Cemetery, and Creevykeel Court Tomb, County Sligo*
County Sligo, in northwest Ireland, is a landscape rich in archaeological remains, ranging from single standing stones and raised beaches, to burial monuments castles, and holy wells. The Cúil Irra (Coolrea) peninsula, near Sligo town, is home to several important Neolithic sites, including Knocknarea Mountain and the Carrowmore Megalithic Cemetery. These sites are among the earliest of the Irish Megalithic tradition yet recorded. Radiocarbon dates from the Carrowmore site, suggest the earliest tombs may have been constructed as early as 4300 BCE, or 6,300 years ago.

Knocknarea is a large, 327-metre-high, limestone mountain, which commands a visually-stunning focus over the landscape of the Cúil Irra peninsula. Even though it is smaller than Uluru, or Ayers Rock, in Australia, in appearance Knocknarea is very similar. Atop the vast flat peak, is the huge Neolithic stone mound known as Miosgán Medbha (Maeve's Tomb). Formal excavation has never been undertaken here, but it is thought to be a large passage tomb of the order of those at the Brú na Bóinne. Maeve's Tomb is roughly fifty-five meters in diameter, and eleven meters in height, and is made from locally-quarried limestone, which is likely to have come from an area on the mountain itself. There are remains of many smaller passage tombs across the landscape of Knocknarea, as well as hut sites, and a large embanked area along the eastern slope. It is thought the passage tombs and other remains may have been constructed in around 3000 BCE.

Knocknarea Mountain, from the Carrowmore Megalithic Cemetery, in County Sligo. Just visible on the horizon, is the passage tomb on the plateau of the mountain.

Stefan Burgh, of National University of Ireland, Galway (NUIG), has referred to Knocknarea as the, 'ultimate monument' (2002: 139). The summit was accessible from the eastern slope, where today's visitors also must ascend. Steep cliffs on all other sides would make the approach difficult, or nearly impossible. The tomb itself is also most visible from the eastern approach, further suggesting that Neolithic people expected it to be seen and accessed from the east. Burgh, who headed the Knocknarea Archaeological Project, found extensive evidence of Neolithic life on the mountain. The twenty or so hut sites indicate that the people who were building the tombs, were also living on the mountain, at least during periods of construction. Long, winding banks along the eastern ridge, may have been used to separate the sacred space of the burials, from the living spaces further along the mountain, much the way George Eogan understands the quartz paving at Knowth. Burgh also suggests the location of the banks along the eastern ridge, may have served as a pathway toward the monuments, and further enhanced the visual impact of the transformed landscape of the mountain (2002).

Maeve's Tomb, at Knocknarea Mountain.

The Cúil Irra and Ox Mountains from Knocknarea. This extraordinary landscape has been exploited and worshipped by people from the Early Neolithic.

As with all fragile remains of the past, Maeve's Tomb, and the mountain itself, have been subject to an increasing amount of foot traffic and damage due to visitors climbing the tomb, and removing stones as souvenirs. Visitors may be unaware of the damage they are doing to the landscape when they remove stones, or likewise, when they bring stones to place on the tomb, as local legend suggests visitors do, 'in order to keep Maeve safely buried'. On more than one occasion, visitors have moved the limestone of the huts and tombs, to spell out their own initials in huge letters on the top of the mountain. Archaeologists and caretakers from the Carrowmore Megalithic Cemetery have had to carefully replace them, once made aware of the vandalism. There are no signs reminding visitors to respect the landscape and monuments, but it is hoped that all visitors will refrain from climbing on the tombs, or removing or adding stones to it.

Carrowmore Megalithic Cemetery was, at one time, an extensive ceremonial landscape, between Knocknarea, and the Ox Mountains on the Cúil Irra peninsula. One of the largest megalithic cemeteries in Europe, there are thirty visible tombs, of the sixty-five to one hundred thought to have existed at one time. Many tombs have been damaged or destroyed in modern times, due to farming, road building, and reuse in the construction of farm buildings in the local area. Carrowmore is also among the most ancient of megalithic sites in Ireland, with radiocarbon dates indicating construction from about 4500 to 3500 BCE. The structures are mostly 'dolmen circles', which are small dolmens, encircled by large upright and recumbent stones. The central tomb, called Listoghil, has been extensively excavated and reconstructed in the recent past, by the Office of Public Works. It is a large cairn, covering another dolmen, which is now exposed for public access. This is an unusual structure and may have been the final tomb constructed on the site, around 3600 BCE. Its size seems to indicate that it was a focal point for the people who inhabited the surrounding landscape and used the tombs. All the tombs are constructed of local gneiss, which was likely to have been mined from the nearby Ox Mountains.

Most of the small tombs, which stretch out across the Carrowmore landscape, contained cremated human remains, and there is little indication that any of the smaller dolmen circles had a stone cairn covering. Listoghil itself contained many burials, both cremations and inhumations. The skeletal remains indicate the remains underwent a complex ritual of preparation, including excarnation, or de-fleshing, in which the body would be left to decay, and then would be either cremated, and placed inside the tomb, or would be inhumed in the tomb.

Access to Carrowmore is through the Visitor's Centre, a short drive from Sligo town, where guided tours may also be booked. Many of the sites, are also located away from the central site surrounding Listoghil, and can be found across the road, on OPW property, adjacent to the Sligo Equestrian Centre, and down a side road in a number of farmer's fields. Always ask permission from the farmers or landowners before accessing these sites. Knocknarea can be seen from nearly every vantage point at Carrowmore, as well as a number of other mountain top tombs in the hills surrounding the cemetery.

Creevykeel Court Tomb is located a short distance from Sligo, on the main Sligo–Bundoran road. It is one of the best remaining examples of a court tomb in Ireland. It overlooks a natural harbour, near Mullaghmore, County Sligo and is one among many that seem to be clustered between Sligo, and Donegal Bay to the north; over 400 court tombs are known in Ireland, and fewer than ten exist south of the Dundalk-Galway line. Court tombs are not unique to Ireland; they can be found from Poland in the east, to Ireland in the west.

A degraded tomb at Carrowmore Megalithic Cemetery.

Dolmen with kerb stones at Carrowmore Megalithic Cemetery; Knocknarea Mountain visible in background.

Dolmen at Carrowmore Megalithic Cemetery; Knocknarea Mountain visible in background.

Court tombs may be the earliest megalithic monuments in Ireland, and seem to have been part of the first agricultural communities' traditions. Creevykeel dates to between 4000 and 2500 BCE. It is a classic example of the court tomb, with a large, open, circular court at one end, where mourners and others may have gathered, leading to a long, trapezoidal, covered gallery, with a very narrow entrance to house the dead. Creevykeel seems to have been added to and rebuilt over the course of its use, but it retained its main function as a burial place during the Neolithic. As with most known court tombs in Ireland, it has an east-west orientation and is built of dry-stone. Creevykeel's court is approximately fourteen by nine meters, and this leads into a short (nine meter) narrow passage, which is divided into a front and back area, with set stones. Entrance to the court itself is through an equally narrow passage, giving the visitor the feeling of entering a liminal space, different from the outside world. A smaller and later chamber was added on the western end of the tomb, on the southern facing side. It is thought the tomb may have measured close to sixty meters in length, and over twenty-five meters in width when it was completed, but much of it had been damaged and destroyed, prior to the excavation and restoration undertaken in the 1930s (Waddell 2000, Harbison 1994). Four cremation burials were found in shallow pits within the gallery, and one had a small flint scraper associated with it (Harbison 1994). Several other artefacts were also recovered, including Neolithic pottery, a stone bead, polished stone axes, scrapers, and flint arrowheads.

The entrance of the Creevykeel Court Tomb, in County Sligo.

The large 'court' at Creevykeel, taken from the burial chamber.

*Left*: Looking out from the burial chambers, across the court, and toward the tomb entrance at Creevykeel.

*Below:* The massive stonework used to divide the burial area, or place of the dead, from the court, a place of ceremony and life at Creevykeel.

The massive rubble walls and interior orthostats of the Creevykeel Court tomb.

*Carrowkeel, County Sligo*

To the south and east of Carrowmore, Knocknarea, and Creevykeel, is the third of the four great megalithic cemeteries of Ireland, that of Carrowkeel in the Bricklieve Mountains. More than a dozen cairns are dramatically situated on high ground overlooking Lough Arrow, and many of these are believed to be passage tombs. Visible from this grouping of tombs, is Knocknarea on the horizon. One of the tombs was also constructed with a roof box similar to the one at Newgrange. The cemetery was partially, and unscientifically, excavated in the early part of the twentieth century, and little work has been done there since. Several of the accessible tombs have cruciform and other type passages, and many produced a variety of artefacts, including bits of Carrowkeel pottery, bone pins, beads, pendants, a boar's tusk, and stone balls (Waddell 2000). When the tombs were initially investigated in the early 1900s, they were still covered with a thick layer of turf, none of which remains today. Few of the tombs are able to be visited today, as many are located on private lands across the peaks. The four that are most reachable are under a high degree of stress, due to their unprotected nature. Visitors climb the tombs, dislodging the cairns' coverings, carve their names on the interior orthostats, and often leave rubbish behind after their visits. On one occasion, when I was photographing the site for this publication, I asked several tourists to come down off one of the tombs, only to be told to mind my own business, and that there were no signs saying they couldn't do so. I asked if there were signs in the cemetery where their ancestors were buried stating the same thing, and I was greeted with laughter and blank stares. Ignorance, it seems, is universal. Again, as with all fragile, ancient sites, treat Carrowkeel with respect and great care when visiting. Further damage to sites of this calibre may lead to them being closed to all visitor traffic.

One of the massive passage tombs that compose the Neolithic landscape of Carrowkeel and Keshcorran, in County Sligo.

Lough Arrow from Carrowkeel. This body of water (and Lough Key to its east) was an area of ceremonial and ritual activity from the early Neolithic.

Three of the tombs at the Carrowkeel Megalithic Cemetery.

Front view of passage tomb at Carrowkeel. When first explored in the twentieth century, the tombs retained their turf coverings, none of which remain today. Visitors to these isolated sites often climb on the fragile tombs, carve their initials into the ancient structures, take away 'souvenir' stones, or leave rubbish and 'offerings' behind. These activities only help to speed the destruction of these incredible sites, and, in turn, hasten the destruction of Ireland's heritage.

*Left:* Tomb G, at Carrowkeel, has a 'roof box' similar to that of Newgrange.

*Below:* Knocknarea Mountain and Maeve's Tomb are visible in the far distance, from the roof box of Tomb G.

Carrowkeel cemetery is located off the main Dublin-Sligo road (N4), just north-west of Boyle, in the townland of Castlebaldwin, and is well sign-posted. Please remember to close all gates you drive through as you approach the site. Four-wheel-drive vehicles, and cars can park close to the site, after traversing a very steep and winding road. Other vehicles, including people carriers, campers and recreational vehicles, and buses, should park in the upper car park as posted, and visitors should continue on foot. Also in the area, are the Keshcorran complex and the Heapstown cairn, as well as a large assortment of Neolithic, Bronze Age, and Iron Age sites, located near Lough Arrow.

*Loughcrew, County Meath*
There are four great megalithic cemeteries in Ireland: the Brú na Bóinne, Carrowmore, Carrowkeel, and Loughcrew. Like the others, Loughcrew is located on high ground, in this case, on three peaks in the Slieve na Cailleach (Hills of the Hag), near Oldcastle, in County Meath. Locally known as Carnbane East, Carnbane West, and Patrickstown Hill, there are more than 20 passage tombs and cairns across the visible landscape, including the slopes and hillocks between, and among, the three main peaks. The views from the peaks are breathtaking, and it is easy to understand why the people of the area chose the site, over 5,000 years ago, to bury their honoured dead. Carnbane East and West are dominated by enormous central tombs, which are surrounded by smaller satellite tombs. The tombs on Carnbane East are the most visited of the three peaks and most easily accessible. None of the tombs retains their turf covering, and most of the tombs have also lost their cobbles, and their corbelled roofs as well (the exception being the largest of the tombs), and are now open to the elements. The passage tombs and cairns at Loughcrew are highly decorated, the most visible decorations are in the large, covered tombs, where the elements have not worn them away. The Office of Public Works has only recently taken an interest in preserving the site; their lack of attention to them in the past is obvious, by the damage that has been done to the exterior tombs, and to the artwork in the interior passages of the tombs.

During the Neolithic, people were very conscious of the changes in season, the equinoxes, and the solstices; their lives depended on knowing when to plant and harvest, when to expect their sheep and cattle to begin lambing and calving, and when to slaughter their herds. The solstices and equinoxes – which occur about 20 March, 21 June, 22 September, and 21 December – are what the Irish calendar is based upon. Most countries base their seasons on the Roman

The central tomb (T) at Carnbane East, with Cairn U to the left, at the Loughcrew Megalithic Cemetery, near Oldcastle, in County Meath.

*Above left:* Cairn U, one of the several satellite tombs at Carnbane East. Loughcrew Megalithic Cemetery is located on three peaks called the Slieve na Cailleach (Hills of the Hag) at Patrickstown, Carnbane East, and Carnbane West. Carnbane East and West both have large central tombs, circled by smaller satellite tombs, much like the later formation at Knowth.

*Above right:* Cairn V with its large set stone at the entrance. None of the smaller tombs retain their cobble or turf coverings. Because these outer tombs have been left to the elements, much of the rock art recorded over the last 150 years has disappeared. This has accelerated in the last thirty years due to pollutants, such as acid rain, and vandalism.

Cairn S at the back of the massive central tomb T, on Carnbane East. The stones used to construct these tombs are mostly of greywacke, which is a very porous and easily damaged stone.

calendar. In Ireland, spring includes February, March, and April, summer: May, June and July, autumn: August, September and October, and winter: November, December and January. Newgrange, as stated above, is oriented toward the Winter solstice, while the main tomb at Carnbane East (T), is oriented toward the autumnal and spring (or vernal) equinoxes. The light from the equinoxes passes along the passageway floor, into the cruciform chamber, and onto the back stones, before withdrawing quickly back down the passage.

The tombs at Loughcrew are in various states of repair. After more than 5,000 years, many of the cairns have collapsed and cannot be entered safely, but many of them are also open and accessible. The largest of the tombs which retain their cobbled coverings, are kept locked to avoid further damage, but the keys can be obtained from the Loughcrew Gardens during the spring, summer, and autumn (when the OPW is not on site), and from the Loughcrew House Hotel, during the winter for a small deposit. As with all sites in Ireland, care and respect for the landscape must be exercised.

Climbing on the tombs is discouraged, and leaving anything behind (such as rubbish, cigarette butts, your initials, or 'offerings') is disapproved of, and only helps to hasten the degradation of this unique and incredible site.

Loughcrew is best approached from the town of Kells off the N3 motorway. From the town centre, turn left, onto the N52 toward Mullingar, then an immediate right, onto the R168, toward Oldcastle. Loughcrew is sign-posted along the way. It is advised that visitors proceed to the Loughcrew Gardens, which are located beyond the turn-off for the tombs, on the left, in order to inquire about the key and a torch. You must leave identification and a deposit.

*Stone Circles*

The most famous stone circle in the world is the great Stonehenge, on the Salisbury Plain, in England, which was begun over 5,000 years ago and finished about 3,500 years ago. From the Neolithic, and into the Bronze Age, people across Europe were constructing monuments on the landscape, which included large standing stones arranged in circles (such as Stonehenge), rows (like Carnac in France), or as singular markers. People in Ireland were busy constructing these types of monuments as well, and it is likely the change in the style of megalithic monuments, marks a change in culture as well. Stone circles in Ireland, when they can be dated, are mostly erected in the late Neolithic, and into the Bronze Age, when new materials for tools, new social structures, and possibly new languages were being introduced.

View from Cairn S toward the central tomb T.

Front view of Cairn T at Carnbane East. This huge cruciform passage tomb is filled with rock art down the entire passage and in all three burial chambers. Most passage tombs in Ireland also have corbelled roofs, which consist of massive flat stones, stacked and angled in such a way as to support the enormous weight of the turf and rubble covering, and to keep out the damp. Cairn T is kept locked, and can only be opened with permission.

When stone circles and standing stones appeared on the landscape, passage tombs containing the remains of many people, fell into disuse, and there was an increase in the use of burial tombs and barrows for a single elite member of society.

There are hundreds of stone circles and alignments in Ireland, with concentrations in Munster and Ulster, and a scattering of anomalous and unrelated sites over the rest of the country. In Munster, this dramatic shift in building style may be directly related to the presence of copper mines on Ross Island, in Kerry, and Mount Gabriel in Cork which were first utilized, between 2400 and 2000 BCE (O' Brien 1996). In many cases, the stone monuments are found in clusters, creating an entire landscape of ritual or ceremonial sites. Stone circles, alignments, and standing stones were part of a new tradition of complex manipulation of the landscape, by a much more densely settled population. Tree ring analysis suggests that there was a shift in climate around the time these changes take place, with colder and wetter conditions, and a rapid increase in bog development. Henge monuments, or monuments encircled with ditched and banked enclosures, also began appearing on the landscape, and there is more evidence of man-made landscapes surrounding the monuments. Pottery styles and tool production changed, and increased farming activity over the preceding millennia, resulted in a dramatic reduction in forest and tree cover. Because of this, settlements and ritual landscapes became highly visible to others, and there is a concomitant increase in defended farmsteads, weaponry, and injuries, which suggest that conflict between tribes was becoming more common.

Rock art in the interior of Cairn T, at the Loughcrew Megalithic Cemetery. As can be seen above right, someone took chalk and charcoal to the intricate designs on the orthostats, ruining the art. Conservators are unable to remove the chalk and charcoal, because removal may further damage the designs.

The Uragh Stone Circle, located on the Beara Peninsula in County Kerry, is a Neolithic, five-stone circle, set on an elevated platform, near the Gleninchaquin Park. Though small, the circle is marked by a very tall (over 3m), single stone which accompanies five smaller ones, one of which is a large, recumbent stone directly in front of the tall, standing stone. The setting of the circle is perhaps its most stunning aspect. Upon the approach to the circle, it remains hidden by the crest of the hill, and it is only when a visitor has climbed to the top of the platform, that the spectacular circle and scenery become clear.

The Uragh Stone Circle, on the Beara Peninsula. This small, five-stone circle is situated against the backdrop of Gleninchaquin Park, in County Kerry. It is also accompanied by a large (3m tall) standing stone.

The Uragh Stone Circle, on the Beara Peninsula, looking northwest.

*Left:* The Uragh Stone Circle, looking north showing the recumbent stone, and a badly tilting stone. The recumbent stone has been placed in front of the large standing stone.

*Below:* The Uragh Stone Circle, on the Beara Peninsula in County Kerry. The Gleninchaquin Falls are clearly visible in the background.

The beautiful Kenmare Stone Circle (known locally as 'Shulberries'), in Kenmare, County Kerry.

View showing the large boulder burial, in the centre of the Kenmare Stone Circle.

Not far from the Uragh Circle, in the town of Kenmare, is a fifteen-stone circle, with a large boulder burial at its centre. This circle (the Kenmare Circle or 'Shulberries') is a Late Neolithic–Early Bronze Age structure, and is of a more sophisticated and well-developed design than the earlier Uragh Circle. It does not have the same dramatic setting however. The Kenmare Circle is not far from an extensive copper deposit, which was used over the transition period, from Neolithic to Bronze Age. There are many stone circles located in this part of Munster, ranging from Limerick to Waterford, but stone circles and standing stones can be found in all areas of Ireland. Exactly why they were constructed, and why the particular places they were built were chosen, may never be known, but scholars have speculated that they may have been territorial markers which were clearly visible on the denuded landscape.

The Kenmare Circle represents the beginning of a new cultural epoch in Ireland. Between 2500 and 2000 BCE, the Bronze Age came to the island, bringing with it new technologies, lifestyles, and new peoples. The discovery and development of metal technologies was to change peoples' lives in a variety of ways, including clearly-defined and defended territories, warrior aristocracies, new religious beliefs, and new weapons and symbols of status.

Many Irish stone circles utilise 'recumbent' stones in the construction. These stones are placed on their sides rather than placed upright. This photograph shows a series of recumbent stones, at the Kenmare Stone Circle.

# FOUR

# THE BRONZE AGE (2200-500 BCE)

In 2200 BCE, the agricultural way of life established over the previous 2,000 years, was firmly in place in Ireland. It was also about this time, that the Irish began to take notice of a new material in use in much of the rest of Europe: copper. This new material, when mixed with tin to make bronze, would revolutionize Europe, in much the same way agriculture had. The exploitation of copper in mines, such as those found at Ross Island, in Killarney, County Kerry, and Mount Gabriel, County Cork, also began in earnest around 2000 BCE (O'Brien 1994). Perhaps more importantly, the smiths who worked the copper and tin, also found an unrivalled talent in working gold. Ireland today boasts one of the largest, and most important collections of Bronze-Age gold artefacts in Western Europe, at the National Museum of Archaeology, on Kildare Street, Dublin.

It is very difficult to pinpoint the exact time when Ireland is considered to have entered the Bronze Age. Most archaeologists would agree that the shift toward a metal-using economy, began between 2200 and 1800 BCE. As with the Neolithic, it took some time before the entire population made both the material and cultural changes commonly associated with the Bronze Age. In Ireland the use of stone tools also continued well into the Bronze Age, with both materials coeval on most sites of the period. Bronze and gold were materials that symbolised high status, especially in the Early Bronze Age, whereas common folk were still highly-dependent upon the stone tools, and lithic resources of Neolithic. The Bronze Age was to transform Europe, with new social orders, religions, settlement patterns, economies, and technologies (Kristiansen and Larsson 2005).

## TRADE

As the Neolithic drew to a close, trade across Ireland among the Stone Age tribes was well established. Late Neolithic people had also begun to trade for materials further afield; artefacts and raw materials from Britain and the continent begin to appear in the archaeological record with some degree of expectation. Bronze objects, as well as high-quality copper ore and tin, were highly-sought after goods, much of which could only be acquired through foreign trade. While copper is a local material in Ireland, tin, a necessary component in the making of bronze, is very rare. Bronze Age people in Ireland, traded for British tin, as well as for tin from the Iberian Peninsula and, other continental sources. Trading for other goods such as cattle, horses, decorative materials, and food was also common. Craftspeople would also become entrepreneurial in the Bronze Age, often travelling long distances, plying their trade and expertise. Because of this, the use of bronze, copper, and tin, as well as that of gold and silver, spread very quickly throughout Europe.

## METALS

The introduction of bronze into the toolkit of the Irish tribes, enabled the emergence of an elite class, who would display their items as symbols of their rank and status. Bronze is a highly-malleable material which can be shaped into countless weapons, ornaments, and household goods. Unlike stone tools, which have a tendency to break, bronze tools can be resharpened, re-hammered, or melted down, and made again. Irish smiths quickly learned how to fashion high-quality tools and weapons from bronze, and established a new and highly valued specialisation.

Gold also came into fashion in the Bronze Age, and was often combined with copper, in order to both strengthen a piece and to give it a deep sheen. Ireland has numerous sources of gold, including Wicklow, where nuggets could be panned from rivers and streams. Decorative personal ornaments such as lunula, gorgets, torcs, lock rings, bracelets, dress pins, and earrings were fashioned for the elite classes. Goldsmiths in Ireland were highly-accomplished, and their fine *repoussé* and incised work on these items, is among the most beautiful and intricate known from the period.

## ELITES

An elite class emerged in the Bronze Age. Unlike the Neolithic and Mesolithic periods, where leadership and merit were valued, wealth and power became important attributes in the Bronze Age. Though still organised into tribes, social stratification and hierarchical organization become more obvious in the archaeological record. Large round houses, often with palisaded-defensive works, are found, often with smaller, less grand houses on their periphery. Archaeological evidence found within, and among, house remains indicate that these large houses were likely to have been inhabited by tribal elites; leaders whom the surrounding members answered to, protected, and followed. During the Bronze Age, tribes also constructed hill and promontory forts, where it is believed elite members of the tribe lived.

## SOCIETY

In the Bronze Age, new status and prestige goods make their way into the archaeological record. Daggers, different types of swords, personal ornaments, and household wares, such as metal cups and cauldrons, begin to demonstrate a polarisation of classes among tribal peoples. An aristocratic class emerges, which supersedes the meritocracy of the Neolithic. Social ranking is less fluid, and this social elitism is tied to new ideas of wealth, value, and exchange. Though less visible in Ireland, 'princely graves' appear throughout much of the rest of Europe, with rich accoutrements such as gold ornaments, weapons, household goods, sacrificed animals, and sometimes sacrificed humans, accompanying the honoured dead. In Ireland, the wealth of some Bronze Age tribal leaders is most evident in the rich, gold hoards found throughout the island and the large earthen enclosures, hill forts, and round houses of the period (see below). Throughout much of Europe and the Near East, the beginning of the Bronze Age also marks the beginning of early state-formation, writing systems, organised military units, and urbanisation (Kristiansen and Larsson 2005). In Ireland, these would not become part of Bronze Age culture, and, in some cases, such as urbanisation, would not become part of Irish life for another 2,000 years.

## COSMOLOGY

During the Neolithic period, social elites are thought to have been cremated and buried within the passage tombs, and other burial chambers which dot the landscape. In the Bronze Age, the use of large tombs falls out of favour. Single graves (often in the form of cist burials) become the norm, with most burials being inhumations, rather than cremations in the early Bronze Age. Large, flat cemeteries containing many individuals, relatives, or tribal members, also become common. It is thought this tradition came from the Urnfield Peoples of central Europe. Elites were commonly buried in barrows, which were raised ditch and bank enclosures with a cist burial or burials in the centre. In Ireland, understanding Bronze Age cosmological belief is hampered, by what John Waddell has called a, 'bewildering variety of funerary ritual' (1990: 1), in the 1300+ known Bronze Age burials. As Waddell makes clear there is an enormous array of evidence:

Unburnt burials
Cremated burials
Cist graves
Pit graves
Tumuli
Flat graves
Cemeteries
Single graves
Grave goods
No grave goods

All of this suggests new belief systems and understandings of the world. Ritual deposits (votive offerings) are also more commonly found during the Bronze Age, suggesting a plethora of gods and spirits, who needed constant placation; in the Neolithic a send-off at death, and a consideration of the seasons was a pre-occupation; in the Bronze Age the world seems to have become a bigger and much more complex place, filled with vast realms of otherworldly uncertainty.

Ritual and ceremonial areas also emerge in the Bronze Age. Votive offerings such as those mentioned above, were deposited in areas of special significance, such as streams, bogs, ponds, rivers, and lakes. In Armagh, the King's Stables, a large artificial pond roughly coeval with Haughey's Fort was constructed.

Tech Cormaic at Tara is an example of a ring barrow, widely used in the Bronze Age in Ireland. Ring barrows vary in size, but are characterised by a small burial plot (often a cist burial) in the centre, surrounded by a bank and ditch (or fosse).

During excavation several votive offerings were recovered, including clay, casting moulds for bronze, leaf-shaped swords, bits of pottery, 'five red deer antlers, the skulls of several dogs and part of a human skull' (Lynn 2003: 54). The human skull was limited to the facial bones, which had been purposefully hacked from the rest of the skull. More than 200 animal bones were found, including those of red deer, cattle, dogs, pigs, sheep, and other unidentified species.

## SETTLEMENTS

The farmsteads and small hamlets of the Neolithic, gave way to open villages across the landscape of Ireland. The villages, though small on any scale, indicate that people were living in relative comfort, and in both extended and nuclear families. House-size, and the artefacts found within them, and in the vicinity of them, also indicate status; few would have been of high rank, a number would have been specialised craftspeople, many would have been farmers, and some were slaves and lower-class individuals. Later in the Bronze Age, a warrior aristocracy developed, shown through an explosion of weaponry, armour, and conflict injuries visible on skeletal remains. Warriors may have lived among the villagers, but may have spent a good deal of their time in the fortified hilltop settlements which began to appear in the Early and Middle Bronze Age. In Ireland, large, earthen enclosures also began to appear, such as Haughey's Fort, in Armagh, Rathnadavre in the Crúachain complex, in Roscommon, Dún Ailinne in Kildare, and Maeve's Fort in Meath near Tara. It is unclear what function these large enclosures may have had, as there is a lack of consistency in what is revealed in excavation; some seem to have held round houses, others may have been strictly for ritual gatherings; some suggest they were used as cattle pens, while others contain burials. Haughey's Fort seems to have served a number of purposes. James Mallory excavated there for several seasons from 1987-1995, and discovered that the 'fort' was occupied in the Late Bronze Age (about 1100-900 BCE), contained numerous storage pits, had post holes indicating a palisade or stockade-like enclosure, and was surrounded by two concentric ditches. Among the more unusual finds recovered by Mallory, and his team, were the skulls of two enormous dogs, and bones from domesticated animals, that were also unusually large for the time (Lynn 2003). A cup-and-ring marked stone found on the hilltop of the fort, combined with the burial of these large animals, suggests Haughey's Fort may have been used for ceremonial purposes during the Bronze Age.

Defended complexes also become more evident, such as Dún Aenghus, on Inis Mór, in the Aran Islands (which Ó Faoláin 2004 refers to as a settlement). Dún Aenghus is a very large, triple-walled, dry stone fort, located on the very edge of a cliff on Inis Mór. Excavation at the site has revealed a Bronze Age date of occupation. The fort is surrounded on three sides by a *chevaux de frise*, a wall of sharp stones, angled outward toward anyone approaching the fort from the landward sides. Sites such as Dún Aenghus indicate that warfare and the protection of territory, became paramount in the Bronze Age.

Density of settlement may be indicated through the proliferation of Fulacht fiadh, enigmatic, horseshoe-shaped mounds of burnt stone, of which over 4,000 have been identified in Ireland. It has been suggested the fulacht were used as cooking stations, but their purpose is not certain. Most fulacht contained a square, or rectangular, stone or wooden box about the size of a coffin which was surrounded by a pile of burnt stones, which over time became covered over with turf. Experimental archaeology has shown that heated stones could be deposited in the water-filled boxes, and meat and other foods then boiled. Recent experiments have also suggested, that fulacht were used to brew beer. Archaeological remains recovered in the form of flora, fauna, and pollen do not come down on either side of the fulacht argument.

## ECONOMY

The Bronze Age brings about the beginnings of the division of labour, and craft specialisation. The division of labour is the separation of a workforce or community into different categories of labour, where everyone involved has specific tasks. In the Bronze Age, this may have meant that farming might have been split into those who raised young stock for slaughter, those who ploughed, planted, and harvested crops, and those who herded sheep and cattle. Craft specialisation is linked with the division of labour, in that specific tasks would be performed by particular people, or classes of people, in a community. Archaeologically, we see this in the recovery of pottery kilns, metal-working areas, farming zones, and other craft and production areas. Once established, there follows the specialised tasks of potters, metal workers, religious leaders, and warriors, as well as slaves who also would have been recognised as a particular class of people who performed particular tasks. This is linked to the growing commodification of metals and ores. On the continent, systems of weights and measures pertaining to metals had come into use and these eventually evolved into standards of trade. Metal became more valued, and in higher demand, and mining intensified throughout ore-producing regions in Europe, the Caucasus, and the Near East. The production and availability of trade goods increased, and with them centres of trade became recognised. The trading centres enabled Irish craftsmen to compete with other craftspeople from Europe and surrounding regions. Trade included finished products, unfinished 'blanks', foods, people, animals, and pottery. Territory and the control of trade routes and waterways, were important aspects of the economy, both on the continent and in Ireland. Currency, in the form of ring ingots, and bars of copper, bronze, tin, and silver, were introduced from the east, as a formal mode of exchange.

## TECHNOLOGY

Once copper was combined with tin to form bronze, new methods of casting, moulding, and creating tools and ornaments soon developed. This 'tin bronze', gave way to specialised workshops and itinerant craftspeople, who had the potential to become wealthy and powerful, once their expertise was recognised. Another evolving technological breakthrough, was the development of spoked wheels, used on lighter horse-pulled chariots, rather than the solid, wooden-wheeled, heavy carts of previous generations. Horse harness, yokes for oxen, ploughs, bits and bridles, and moulded armour also came into being. The demand for luxury goods and weaponry put a strain on specialised production, and soon an early form of mass-production of certain goods (ingots, axes, halberds, and such), emerged with entire peripheries of production being found across Europe and Ireland.

## STONE CIRCLES, ALIGNMENTS, STANDING STONES

The Neolithic period in Ireland, is recognised by the gradual change to an agricultural way of life, from the foraging lifestyle of the Mesolithic. Neolithic peoples also manipulated their landscape through forest clearance, tillage, and pasturage, and the construction of a wide variety of stone monuments, usually related to mortuary ritual and the passage of seasons. In the Bronze Age, passage tombs and other forms of large burial chambers, go out of fashion. We do not know why this occurs; we can only surmise that, as with the rapid spread of bronze, there was an equally rapid spread of new cosmological and religious belief across much of Europe. In Ireland, we observe the gradual disuse of passage tombs over time; in some cases cremation burials within tombs are stopped, but inhumations on the tombs' surface, continues for some time, as at the Mound of Hostages, at Tara. Wedge tombs, the final megalithic burial style of the Neolithic-Bronze Age transition, continue to be used, though in the Early Bronze Age, skeletal remains, rather than cremations, are interred within them.

In the Late Neolithic, stone circles begin to be built in conspicuous areas, such as the Uragh and Kenmare circles, mentioned in the previous chapter. This tradition continues through the Bronze Age, with some stone circles reaching very large proportions. In Lough Gur, County Limerick, the Grange stone circle is the largest extant in Ireland, with 113 stones. Grange and Lough Gur will be returned to below. Stone alignments, which are more than two stones arrayed along a line, rather than on a curve, also crop up and are found across Europe. Many seem to be oriented on solstice or equinox lines, some also seem to be oriented toward monuments, or natural areas, which may have held particular significance for the people who built them, such as the stone alignment and 'Boheh Stone', near Croagh Patrick, in County Mayo. The importance of Croagh Patrick to Bronze Age and earlier people, is attested to by the wide variety of monuments in its vicinity, including the Eanach Choill an Daingin complex (oval enclosure, stone circle, alignment all of Bronze Age date), a Bronze Age wedge tomb, and a fulacht fiadh. On Clare Island, off the coast and within site of Croagh Patrick, many more standing stones, remnants of circles, promontory forts, and fulacht fiadh are also visible. In Ireland, recumbent stone circles seem to have been preferred to circles which only had upright stones, though many upright circles are also found throughout the country.

## SUMMARY

From about 2200 BCE, a new metal-using economy emerges in Ireland. This economy, based on the production of copper, tin, bronze, silver, and gold items also brought with it changes in social organization, religious belief, technologies, and settlement patterns. Social ranking and status, based upon wealth and power, rather than merit and skill, defined the most elite classes of Bronze Age society in Ireland. A warrior class emerged, and as a result, conflict injuries, weaponry, and defensive structures become more common in the archaeological record as the age progresses. Craft specialisation and a division of labour also become apparent as the new economy develops; entrepreneurs, tradesmen, animal breeders, and mercenaries are among those most commonly encountered in Europe at this time. Burial practice undergoes a significant change, from the megalithic culture of the Neolithic. Passage tombs, and other mass cremation graves go out of fashion, replaced by wedge tombs in the Early Bronze Age containing single or multiple inhumation burials, flat cemeteries, cists, barrows, and urn burials, and later, a return to cremations, with and without, grave goods (usually in the form of pottery).

## THE BRONZE AGE TIMELINE IN IRELAND

The first Bronze Age peoples in Ireland were practising an agricultural way of life, much the way their Neolithic predecessors had. The difference was in their toolkit, which now included pieces of copper and bronze. Beginning in around 2200 BCE, knowledge of this new material, and the exploitation of the raw materials needed to produce it, began to spread into Ireland, as trade with Britain and the continent increased contact with cultures already using metals. As the Bronze Age progressed, notions of tribal territoriality, and the need to defend and protect resources increased. Tribes grew larger than in the Neolithic, territories expanded, and leadership became centralised, and was based more on wealth and power than merit. All these changes were directly linked to the new economy, which placed value on items of status such as gold, silver, and bronze objects. By the middle of the Bronze Age in Ireland (1600-1000 BCE), great hoards of valuables were being deposited throughout the land. These hoards included, ring ingots (a form of currency), precious objects of gold and silver, weapons, and symbolic items such as ceremonial axe heads, raw materials, and amber. There may have been a number of reasons for this: they may have been 'stashed' by craftspeople with the intention of re-using them, they may have been buried for safe-keeping, or they may have been votive offerings to the gods of the age. Field systems become permanent, and the hamlets of the countryside become more densely populated. Treatment of the dead was influenced by changes in funerary practice in other areas of Europe: passage tombs and cremation went out of favour; inhumation in single burials or cemeteries emerged, followed by a return to cremation and urn burial. This coincided with a shift away from the tradition of stone circles and henges, and toward religious activities being centred on watery areas, like bogs, lakes and rivers.

Between 1000 and 500 BCE, the Late Bronze Age began its slow transition to the Iron Age. Organised villages and centres of trade were built, territories were marked with standing stones, stone alignments and circles, and the warrior aristocracy of the Bronze Age began to evolve into the chieftain-clan organization of the Iron Age. The turmoil and uncertainty of the period can be demonstrated by the continued use of votive offerings, including that of the massive Dowris Hoard of more than 200 objects, deposited in County Offaly, in around 700 BCE. Dowris included twenty-six bronze horns, swords, socketed axes, razors, an array of carpentry tools, and a huge cauldron. Many archaeologists suggest that the time period may have become progressively more conflict-ridden as the size and occurrence of hoards become more common in the later stages of the Bronze Age. Toward the end of the Bronze Age, there was also a major climatic deterioration, thought to have been brought about by a volcanic eruption in Iceland or some other devastating natural disaster. Temperatures dropped, the climate became wetter, and bog development increased, making entire areas of tillable land unusable. These changes may have been the catalyst for much of the increased conflict and votive offerings in the Late Bronze Age, as people battled for the remaining lands.

## BRONZE AGE SITES IN IRELAND

The archaeology of Bronze Age Ireland is best seen in both the remains on the landscape, and the exquisite displays in the National Museum, on Kildare Street, the Ulster Museum, in Belfast, and in the dozens of local museums throughout the country. The rich artefacts of the period are often more illustrative of the period, than the extant Bronze Age sites, which seem to melt with and dissolve into the preceding Neolithic, and the later Iron Age. Despite the confusion of remains, there are a number which stand out on the landscape, and a few are described below. Driving or hiking directions are given to each. Please use caution when visiting many of these sites, give a few euro when asked, and care for them as you would any national monument.

*Lough Gur, County Limerick*
Lough Gur is a large lake, located between Knockadoon and Knockfennel, in County Limerick, to the south of the city of Limerick. Explorations at Lough Gur and subsequent excavations, have revealed that the area was of great cultural importance over many millennia to the people of the region. Neolithic house platforms, standing stones, ring cairns, ring forts, pillar stones, the Carraig Aille Forts, the Black Castle, wedge tombs, lime kilns, and the Great Stone Circle of Grange are only some of the archaeological remains that span the ages, from the Neolithic, through the medieval period at Lough Gur. Of particular interest to this Bronze Age discussion, are the Lough Gur Wedge Tomb, and the Great Stone Circle of Grange.

The wedge tomb is located on the right, across from the Carraig Aille Stone Forts, as you approach the entrance to the Lough Gur Park. The tomb is quite large and is constructed with one main gallery, one small cist or chamber in the rear of the structure, with a thick-walled gallery, kerb stones, and very large cover or cap stones. When originally excavated, it was found to be greatly disturbed, but contained cremated remains in the rear cist, as well as the inhumed remains of several adults and children, within the main gallery. The bones of cattle and pigs, and pottery were also found within the tomb. According to Waddell, the skeleton of a young ox was found buried a short distance from the tomb, and is believed to be contemporary with it (2000: 97). The remains were radiocarbon dated to between 2500 and 2000 BCE, suggesting that the tomb was in use for several centuries before falling into disuse.

The wedge tomb at Lough Gur, in County Limerick. Wedge tombs were used in the Bronze Age, and are thought to have been the final phase of megalithic burial tomb in Irish prehistory.

A view of the chamber at the wedge tomb at Lough Gur. Several burials were found both within the central chamber, and in the small chamber located at the end of the tomb. The kerbing around the tomb suggests the tomb would have been covered with turf after use.

The Great Stone Circle at Grange is located on the R 512, south of Ballyneety, outside of Limerick City, on the western side of Lough Gur. Excavated in 1939 by Seán P. Ó Ríordáin, the Grange Circle exhibits characteristics of both henge monuments and stone circles, with its thick embankment, into which 113 stones were carefully set. The circle's diameter is about 46m, and the stones are contiguous, rather than set apart as is usual in Irish stone circles. There is a well-defined entrance to the circle, marked by two massive upright stones, as well as several other very large and tall stones, in various locations on the circle. The largest stone is, '2.6m high and [weighs] over 60 tons' (Waddell 2000: 112). There were many associated finds, including flint arrowheads, scrapers, polished stone axes, and hundreds of pottery shards. Two hearths, a few human bones, and some animal bones were also recovered. In an adjoining field, is another smaller and more traditional stone circle, along with a standing stone. The Grange Circle is located on private farmland, but you are welcome to cross over to it providing you use caution. Young cattle are usually grazing nearby, and are very curious when visitors walk through their patch. You will find a small metal box at the entrance, where donations are accepted to assist the owner in the upkeep of fencing, to preserve the area surrounding the monument. Please take care around the monument itself, as it can be very slippery on the best of days.

The entranceway of the huge stone circle at Grange, in County Limerick, showing the large orthostats in the interior. It is unusual among Irish stone circles; it has 113 contiguous stones and is surrounded by a built up bank, like a henge, which the large stones are supported by.

*Above, below and overleaf:* The Grange circle showing the contiguous large stone structure.

*Above:* A more typical Irish stone circle, located in an adjoining field, near the Grange circle. Both of the circles (and a standing stone across the road) are on private land, and are under the care of the family who farm it. Please respect the land and the monuments, and take care when crossing into the area, as young cattle are often grazing near the sites.

The massive Bronze Age fort of Dún Aenghus on Inis Mór in the Aran Islands.

View through the doorway of the fort, looking out across Inis Mór. The fort, like all ancient structures, is a drystone structure, with very thick (3–5m) walls.

A view of Dún Aenghus showing one of the four defensive walls.

To find these monuments, as well the Lough Gur Visitor Centre and Archaeology Park, take the R512 out of Limerick City, through the village of Ballyneety. After four miles, take the second left, after Reardon's Pub in Holycross, the Grange Circle is on the R512 near the pub. Take the first left to Herbertstown and follow signs for Lough Gur. Carraig Aille Forts will be on your left (worth the climb to see these eighth-tenth century structures), and a little further along, the Lough Gur wedge tomb will be on your right. The park is another mile or so on.

*Dún Aenghus, Inis Mór, Aran Islands, County Galway*
The great Bronze Age promontory fort of Dún Aenghus, is located on the largest of the Aran Islands, Inis Mór. The Discovery Programme (Ireland's national archaeology unit) conducted excavations there from 1992-1995. The fort consists of four walls (the outermost is incomplete), enclosing some six hectares of area, in a location, which looms over much of the surrounding landscape. High visibility as well as its elaborate structure, indicate defensive positioning and status were foremost in the inhabitant's minds when they constructed it. Radiocarbon dates suggest the area of the fort was in active use, from about 1300 to 540 BCE. Many of the carbon dates were taken

*Above:* The *chevaux de frise* defensive works which surround Dún Aenghus. The *chevaux de frise* was built of thousands of stones, placed at angles in the ground. Their placement made it very difficult for enemies or other intruders to approach the fort.

*Left:* The promontory cliffs at Dún Aenghus are 100 metres high. Approach from the sea would have been impossible.

from hut sites which pre-date the actual fort. The hut sites may have been used by the people who were building the structure. The innermost structure is a thick-walled fort which is on the edge of a 100-meter-high sea wall. The second and third walls are surrounded with a defensive work called a *chevaux de frise*, which is a jumble of large stones set at angles to impede approach to the fort. Coarse pottery, clay moulds for casting bronze, bronze implements, animal bones, hearths, bone pins, and stone artefacts, indicate the site served a multitude of purposes, not just that of defence.

To reach Dún Aenghus, take the ferry from the mainland; there are a number of ports including Ros á Mhil and Doolin. You can organise transport by bicycle or mini-bus upon arrival. You must walk to the fort from the visitor centre; though not steep, the walkway can be slippery and may have patches of loose stones, so care is required going up and down. Do not cross into sign-posted areas and use extreme caution on the cliff side of the site which is not fenced. High winds are common and visitors can be easily swept over the 300 foot cliffs. Time spent in the visitor centre prior to climbing up to the fort is recommended.

Dún Beag fort on the Dingle Peninsula, in County Kerry. First constructed in the Bronze Age, this promontory fort has been rebuilt several times over many centuries. What remains are ruins of a fort and clochan, from the early medieval period.

Interior, stepped-construction of the massive walls surrounding Dún Beag fort.

*Left:* The drystone walling of the interior clochan at Dún Beag.

*Below:* The promontory to the east of Dún Beag fort. From this vantage point, inhabitants would have seen attackers and others approaching from both sea and land. They also had views of the Skellig Islands, and Blaskets beyond.

The King's Stables, part of the Navan Complex, in County Armagh. This small, man-made ritual pond was constructed in the Bronze Age, and is contemporary with the neighbouring Haughey's Fort.

*Dún Beag (Dunbeg) Promontory Fort, Dingle Peninsula, County Kerry*

A promontory is a mass of land, which overlooks low-lying land or water. Promontories are also commonly referred to as headlands, or peninsulas. A promontory fort is one situated on a cliff of land, either inland, or facing the sea. In the case of Dún Beag (meaning small fort), and Dún Aenghus, the sea serves as natural protection, with built defences only necessary on the landward side of the sites. According to Herity and Eogan, it is 'likely [promontory forts] were introduced from Atlantic Europe' (1977: 227) to Ireland, as the tradition seems to flow from France, Iberia and Britain, and into Ireland. In most cases promontory forts are built on spurs of land, usually with a narrow strip of land connected to the mainland. Banks, ditches, walls, and other forms of defence are then built into and upon the connecting land, to guard against intrusion from the outside. Dún Beag was first constructed in the Late Bronze Age, around 900–800 BCE, based on radiocarbon dates from an early defensive ditch. It shows little evidence of occupation at this time, and much like a similar unoccupied promontory fort at Carrigillihy, in County Cork, the fort's use may have been limited to local protection, or for ceremonial purposes at its earliest stages. At Carrigillihy, remains of houses have been excavated in the local area. The fort at Dún Beag, as it stands today, is a small, defensive structure with massive, thick walls facing the causeway. Entrance to the fort is gained by crossing the ramparts, and ducking through a low doorway, under which a later souterrain can be seen. The walls are fashioned with walkways and steps, making sighting from and defence of the structure efficient. Dún Beag's four lines of banks, five fosses (ditches), and the thick inner dry stone wall are an imposing combination of defensive works for such a small fort. The walled fortification encloses a clochan (possibly a beehive hut), which was probably built during the Early Christian period. The Skelligs and the Blasket Islands can be seen from Dún Beag, and a wide panorama of the surrounding landscape can also be taken in. It is fairly easy to understand why the people of Dingle first built here in the Bronze Age, and why the fort continued to be used over the next 1,000 years or more. To reach Dún Beag, drive through Dingle town, and continue along the coast road (Slea Head Drive), for about 15k. The fort will be on your left, parking is available on the right. If no one is at the small entrance kiosk, please leave a small donation for the upkeep of the site in the box.

*The King's Stables, Armagh, County Armagh*
The Navan Complex in County Armagh includes Emain Macha, Loughnashade, Haughey's Fort, The King's Stables, and a variety of other earthworks, standing stones, and monuments near the city of Armagh. Haughey's Fort, a large enclosed hill fort, and The Kings' Stables, a small, man-made artificial pool, date from the Bronze Age. The King's Stables (so-called because legend suggests the kings of Ulster would bathe and stable their horses there), is a small, 25m-diameter pond located about 700m west of Emain Macha and about 200m east of Haughey's Fort. Until a test excavation was done by Christopher Lynn, in the 1970s, it is likely that the pond had lain nearly undisturbed since it was created nearly 3,000 years before (Lynn 2003). The pond is surrounded by a steep, tree-lined bank on all but the southern side. During excavation Lynn found that the steep sides of the bank, continued to a depth of about 4m to a flat-bottomed pool that, over the millennia, had accumulated a thick layer of fine, silty mud on its bottom, as well a thick mat of vegetation on the water's surface. Excavation of a small section of the pool's bottom revealed more than 200 animal bones, including the complete skeletons of several dogs. The dogs were articulated in such a way

to suggest they were deposited whole, or possibly were drowned in the pool. Several clay moulds for casting bronze, leaf-shaped swords were found, as were hundreds of shards of Bronze Age pottery. In addition to these was the recovery, of 'the facial portion of a young adult male ... which showed signs of having been deliberately detached in antiquity from the rest of the skull' (Lynn 2003: 54). All of these discoveries indicate that the pool had been used for ritual purposes during the Late Bronze Age, and in Lynn's opinion, the pool would have been used by the same people who were using the site of Haughey's Fort (Lynn 2000). When visiting any of the sites of the Navan Complex, exercise caution, as they are open sites located on farmland (the exception is Emain Macha). Though protected by the Department of Heritage, the lands surrounding the sites are still in use. Travel west from Armagh toward the township of Tray, follow signs for Navan Fort/Emain Macha, then proceed on toward Tray and the King's Stables. It is well sign-posted, and there is a small parking area outside of the site. You must traverse a fenced walkway which crosses through farmland to get to the site. Do not attempt to go down the banks of the pool, and use extreme caution in and around the site. The King's Stables, though small and often overlooked, is a very rare site, and is the only known artificial pool in Europe dating from the Bronze Age.

## A NEW AGE

As the young man found at the bottom of the King's Stables lay dying, a new technology had begun to take hold in Europe. Iron implements and weapons had begun to take over, where bronze had once held sway. Bronze remained a popular and useful material, but over time, was used almost exclusively for decoration and household goods. Iron was harder, easier to manipulate, and less expensive to produce. And it swept across Europe, with the tribal peoples who roamed the landscape. By 500 BCE the Iron Age – the final phase of prehistory in Ireland – had come to Éire's shores.

# FIVE

# THE IRON AGE (500 BCE-AD 500)

When we speak of the Iron Age, we are referring to a period in the past, that straddles the ancient world and recorded history. It is called the Iron Age, because of the introduction of iron to the toolkit commonly used by much of ancient Europe. The Iron Age is generally thought to have begun in Europe sometime between 800 and 700 BCE, and is thought to have found its earliest beginnings in central Europe, in the Salzkammergut of Austria. In the Iron Age, people were very mobile, moving throughout the regions of Europe, settling in new areas, passing along technologies and languages, and often going to war with those who stood in their way. Not all peoples in Europe entered the Iron Age at the same time, rather, the technologies and cultural influences of the time spread slowly across the continent.

In Europe, the ages of man are marked by developments in technology. Later prehistory is marked by the introduction of new metals: first copper, in the Late Neolithic (sometimes called the Chalcolithic or copper/stone age), followed by bronze, around 2500 BCE, and finally iron, sometime in the eighth century BCE. The European Iron Age does not mean that all the peoples who began to use iron were the same culturally. In fact, throughout time, Europeans have always been diverse in culture and language. Despite the differences, the sharing of technology and goods through trade networks, and other forms of exchange, helped to shape the similarities between and among European cultures, from the earliest periods of modern human habitation beginning around 40000 BCE.

## TECHNOLOGY

The Iron Age can be described as a time of intense cultural development in Europe. At the same time that the people of Hallstatt, Austria were refining the production of iron, they were also in contact with Greeks and Etruscans, and other peoples from far-flung areas of Europe, because they mined and traded in salt (Salzkammergut, or 'The Estate of the Salt Chamber', is the salt-producing area of Austria, which ranges from Salzberg, to the Dachstein mountains). Salt was extremely important in the ancient world, because it was used to preserve food, especially meats. As the salt miners traded salt with other peoples, their knowledge of iron making, and their iron goods were, likewise, traded. Thus, the new metal was soon found throughout much of Europe. It was used for a variety of purposes, some agricultural (iron wheel rims, plough blades, scythes and sickles), and some household (knives, meat forks, cauldrons, fire dogs), but largely, the new metal, was incorporated into weapons such as swords, spear points, helmets, shields, and arrowheads.

Iron revolutionised life in Europe. It was stronger than bronze, more cost effective, and iron ore was widely available throughout much of the continent. Even today in the twenty-first century, iron is produced on an industrial scale in more than half the countries of the European Union. When combined with carbon, iron could also be made into steel, which is considerably stronger than iron. In the Iron Age, the production of charcoal would have been vital, in order to heat smelting ovens to the high temperatures necessary to produce iron. Niall Kenny has found extensive evidence of long-term, charcoal production throughout Ireland. Iron mining is thought to have been in Ireland since at least the early centuries BC, and likely, prior to that. There are references to iron being extracted from mines, near Lough Allen in County Leitrim, in some of the ancient tales, such as those which refer to Goibniu, a smith of the legendary Tuatha de Danann.

## COMMUNITIES AND SETTLEMENTS

Iron Age people lived in small, settled communities with communal lands, usually not far from their tribal leader. Their culture is generally felt to have been agricultural, with an abundance of domestic livestock, including sheep, goats, pigs, cattle, and horses. Their houses were usually round, with a large, single room and a hearth located in the centre. The roofs were thatched, and were tall and conical. There have also been a number of rectangular house patterns recovered, with small rooms on either end of a large central room, where the hearth was located. The houses could be built of a number of materials, including stone and wattle and daub (woven twigs covered with a mixture of clay, manure, and straw), wood was also likely to have been used, though there are very few remains of wooden buildings due to decay. In many cases, the houses would be surrounded by a bank and ditch, and could also have a palisade for defence. Iron Age people were organised into chiefdoms, with clear leadership, and separate classes of people, who would have specialised in craft production, industry (such as farming), religion, and battle.

Archaeologically, the Iron Age in Ireland is a bit of an enigma. We know it happened, we find bits and pieces of it in the archaeological record. But it seems to have developed along a different timeline than the rest of Europe. Iron was not as commonly used in Ireland as it was in the rest of Europe, until much later in the age, around 100 BCE. While trade continued to be highly-organised and took place between Ireland, Britain and across the continent, the culture of the Iron Age does not seem to have taken hold in Ireland until quite late; even then, it was quite different from how it manifested itself in other parts of Europe.


## TRIBAL LIFE IN AN IRISH CHIEFDOM

Iron Age tribes could be quite large, and were often combined in times of war. It could be difficult to maintain alliances among Iron Age peoples, because leadership was usually not inherited, but based on ability – if a leader failed in conquest, or in their efforts to protect the tribe, they would be deposed and another would take their place. It is known, that women as well as men could serve as chieftain, and could be understood as a people's king or queen. Queen Boudicca of the Iceni in Britain is one of the best known queens of an Iron Age tribe. She was powerful enough to lead several tribes against the Romans in the mid-first century AD. She and her army defeated the Roman legions, at both Colchester and London, then sacked and burned both cities. The Irish tribes are known to have engaged in battle, and would have had a 'warrior aristocracy', with leaders being those who could best protect the chief's interests, through both battle and diplomacy. They were pagans, believing in numerous gods and goddesses, worshipping at streams, wells, springs, glens, forests, and clearings.

The cultures of Iron Age Europe also shared a similar material culture. Beginning in the Hallstatt period (800-450 BCE), the material culture of the most influential peoples of Europe began to be traded extensively across the continent. Pottery styles, weapons, tools, saddlery, and decorative jewellery exhibit classic stylistic associations that archaeologists refer to as Hallstatt style. The La Téne period, which runs from 450 BCE, until the Roman conquest in most areas of Europe, is recognised as a period of genuine creative flourescence among the Iron Age peoples of Europe. Named after the site of La Téne on Lac Neuchatál in Switzerland, the period is an exemplar of the artistic nature of the time. Symmetrical, vegetal styles of decoration appear on everything, from brooches, to pottery, to weaponry. War, and the expansion and movement of larger groups of people, became commonplace as smaller, less influential tribes and cultures were pushed aside, destroyed, or absorbed into the more powerful groups crossing the continent.

In Ireland, tribes would have been organised in a social hierarchy, led by a single elite chief whose word was law. The chief's power is believed to have been tempered, through consultation with war leaders and religious leaders who may have met in counsels to advise the chief, who is also referred to as a 'king' in some literature. Religious leaders would have been part of the most elite of the age, and would have advised the king on matters pertaining to worship, ritual, social gatherings, and the carrying out of sentences on those accused of crimes. War leaders would have advised on alliances, enemies, the training of warriors, and battle strategies. Specialised craftspeople also would have been part of the upper classes. Farmers, those who tended animals, builders, and others would have made up the middle classes. Lower-class individuals may have been conscripts, labourers, and finally slaves, and those unable to contribute to the group's wellbeing.

Much of the day to day life of the tribe members would have been taken up with subsistence: farming and stock rearing being the most important. Seasonal gatherings are thought to have taken place throughout Ireland. These brought many of the far-reaching tribes together to trade, celebrate, conduct business, solidify alliances, and for marriages. The Óenach Tailten was an annual assembly, for racing and athletic contests, held at Teltown (or Tailteann), County Meath, not far from Kells, and the Hill of Tara. It lasted for a week, around 1 August, the feast day of the god Lug, and is also known as Lughnasa. It is believed the King at Tara would have presided over these celebrations, and that marriages would also have been negotiated and performed during the festival. Óenach would have been held throughout Ireland, each within its own territory, though the one at Tailteann is best known. It is referred to in many ancient texts, and celebrations continued there well into the eighteenth century, when they were banned by the church.

As the peoples of Europe jockeyed for position, in Rome, a new highly-organized, politically-motivated machine began to assert itself throughout the peninsula of what is now Italy. First challenging the Greeks and Etruscans to Mediterranean supremacy, the Romans then crossed the Alps into greater Europe, in the first century BCE, forever changing the face of the continent. With few exceptions, the cultures of Iron Age Europe, who had held sway for nearly eight centuries, including the La Téne tribes, the Goths, the Teutons, the Greeks, and others, were defeated, or made allegiant to the new empire that was Rome. One of those exceptions, was the people of the island of Ireland, who observed the legions from the safety of their own shores.

## THE IRISH IRON AGE

The time, when the Irish Bronze Age becomes the Iron Age, is difficult to define. Unlike much of the continent of Europe, Ireland enjoyed relative isolation from the turmoil, which is the hallmark of the period in the rest of Europe. The people traded with other Europeans, and travelled throughout Europe, but, for the most part, they remained out of the fray, left to create their own version of the age. Archaeologically, the Irish Iron Age lacks the familiar markers of the continental Iron Age, until quite late in the era. Occasional Hallstatt materials have been found (such as brooches, swords, and other weapons), but it is not until the La Téne period is in full swing elsewhere, that it can be said a true Irish Iron Age becomes visible – even then, much of what is recovered in the archaeological remains, seems to indicate a simple and subtle evolution in Bronze Age styles.

The Bronze Age, which has such a strong archaeological presence in Ireland, seems to slowly shift toward the Iron Age, many centuries after the rest of Europe (including Ireland's trading partners) is fully committed to it. Sometime between 500 and 250 BCE, iron artefacts, and Iron Age pottery begin to be found in small quantities in Ireland. Bronze Age house and settlement styles continue, but hillforts and ceremonial areas begin to be visible on the landscape. Chiefdoms would have been similar to the Bronze Age tribes, but as the Iron Age proceeds, the chiefs become more powerful, expand their territories, and Irish 'high kings' emerge.

It is in the first centuries before Christ, with the emergent warrior aristocracies of Ireland, and the cultures that formed around them, that we see the true emergence of an Irish Iron Age. During this time, royal sites, such as the Hill of Tara, Emain Macha (Navan Fort), Rathcroghan (Crúachain), and Dún Ailinne, symbolize the division of the island into large territories similar to today's provinces. In the Iron Age, Ireland had five provinces, including Royal Meath (Mídhe), where Tara, Tailteann, and other important tribal meeting places were located. Tara was the inaugural place of the 'high king' of Ireland, an administrative and ceremonial site, which encompassed an entire landscape far larger than what is now preserved in Meath, and it is at the Hill of Tara, that we begin our exploration of Iron Age Ireland.

*The Hill of Tara, County Meath*
Around the first century BCE, the great tribal houses of Ulster, Connaught, Meath, Leinster, and Munster were in constant conflict. The peoples counted their wealth in cattle and land, and great battles could be waged over herds, grazing areas, or trading districts. Legends emerged from these battles, and were passed on through the generations, finally being written down by Christian monks beginning in the sixth century AD. Among the legends, is the Táin bó Cúailgne (The Cattle Raid of Cooley) which recounts the great war between Queen Medb, and her consort King Ailill of Connaught, and Cúchullain, and the Red Branch Knights of Ulster, during the first century AD. This great war between tribes, centred on the royal sites of Rathcroghan, in the west, and Emain Macha in the north, is believed to have begun over a bull in the Cooley peninsula which Queen Medb coveted, and requested of Ailill. When she was refused, she set out to steal it, thus setting off a sequence of events that led to a great war, and eventually the deaths of Cúchullain, the great bull, and, as interpreted by the monks, the symbolic death of Iron Age life, tribalism, and pagan belief.

Archaeologically, the remains of these great centres of tribal power are still visible on the landscape today. Tara has recently undergone a flurry of archaeological investigation, by The Discovery Programme (Ireland's state archaeological service). Through their use of a multitude of investigative methods, including excavation, remote sensing, and LiDAR, a new picture of the great hill has begun to emerge. LiDAR, which stands for Light Detection and Ranging, is a relatively new technology, that utilises laser pulses for contour mapping, and airborne laser swath mapping (ALSM). Tara itself has been exploited by human groups since at least the

Neolithic. The Mound of Hostages (Duma na nGiall) and other nearly-invisible burial mounds at Tara, were constructed around 5,000 years ago, for the elite members of Late Stone Age society. Cremation burials, grave goods, and carved orthostats were all present in the Mound of Hostages, when first excavated in the early twentieth century; many artefacts are on display in the National Museum on Kildare Street. The hill remained in use as an area of symbolic importance, until its own emergence as an area of central significance to Ireland, in the Iron Age. There are at least four bank and ditch structures visible on the perimeter of the site today, including Ráith Grainne, the two Sloping Trenches (Clóenfherta), Rath of the Synods (Ráith na Senad), and Leary's Fort (Ráith Lóegaire). The interior of the site is demarcated by a low, earthen bank (Ráith na Ríg) which encloses the Mound of Hostages, the Forradh and Tech Cormaic (Cormac's House). Between Rath Grainne, and the Mound of Hostages, are the Banqueting Hall (Tech Midchúarta) (actually a cursus, or defined walkway) and the Rath of the Synods. Remote sensing has indicated numerous structures including palisades, additional 'forts' and mounds, and a continuance of the cursus running from its visible terminus, and toward the Mound, and Forradh. The Lia Fáil (or crowning stone), is now located at the centre of the Forradh, but is believed to have originally been erected in front of the Mound of Hostages, much like the standing stones in front of the entrances at Knowth.

The Mound of the Hostages, a Neolithic passage tomb at the Hill of Tara, County Meath. This small tomb was used for thousands of years, from the Neolithic through the Bronze Age.

The single decorated orthostat, immediately to the left of the entrance at the Mound of the Hostages.

Conor Newman, of the National University of Ireland, Galway, organised Tara into a series of phases, beginning in the Neolithic. At this time, a possible palisaded enclosure, pre-dating the Mound of Hostages, was constructed in around 3000 BCE, which may have had ritual significance. Following shortly after this, the people of Tara began to build the Mound of Hostages. Excavations have revealed a ritual burning of the ground surface, two cremation burials outside the tomb prior to building, and a series of pit fires, which surrounded the tomb, all of which have been radiocarbon dated to between 2875 and 1940 BCE. The Mound of Hostages itself, is a small passage tomb, with a decorated orthostat. It contained many cremation burials within the tomb. The continued importance of the passage tomb, is shown through the discovery of forty Bronze Age burials in the mound surface, and within the passage itself. Two burials within the tomb and one on the surface, were inhumations, the rest were cremations.

The third phase Newman suggests, was the building of the Banqueting Hall or Tech Midchúarta, 'between the middle of the fourth and middle of the third millennium BC' (Newman 1997: 227). This large cursus feature may have led to the Neolithic complex. It is constructed of two parallel earthen banks, about 230m long, running north–south, which slope away from the Ráith na Ríg. Several small mounds, rings, and other features are located in the meadow west of the banks. Two of the low profile barrows are still visible west of the monument.

The misnamed 'Banqueting Hall' at the Hill of Tara, is actually a high-banked cursus, or ceremonial walkway, which would have guided visitors to the Hill toward the Ráith na Ríg.

The Ráith na Ríg, or Fort of the King, which surrounds the Forradh, Mound of Hostages and Tech Cormaic, at Tara.

The Forradh, showing the Lia Fáil, and the 1798 commemoration stone. The Forradh is believed to have been a ceremonial site for the high kings of Ireland.

In the Bronze Age, Maeve's Fort, a large embanked enclosure, south of today's Hill of Tara complex was built, and the Bronze Age burials associated with the Mound of Hostages, were interred. Newman indicates the four barrows in the outer bank of the Tara complex, and the ring ditches may also be of Bronze Age date.

The Iron Age is the final prehistoric period of activity at the Hill of Tara. It began with the construction of the Ráith na Ríg, the 300 by 250m embanked enclosure, which encloses more than 55,000 square metres. The ditch, or fosse, associated with the enclosure, was more than 3.5m deep and was surrounded by a palisade. The enclosure was structured in such a way as to incorporate many older monuments within it. Many of the monuments are no longer visible on the ground surface, having been destroyed by ploughing and other farming activities. A flat cemetery in the area of the Rath of the Synods was also in use at this time. The Forradh may also have been built during this period. It is an 87-metre diameter, steep-sided mound, surrounded by two high banks, and two ditches. An accurate date for the Forradh has not been ascertained, because it has not been excavated; some speculate that it may pre-date the Ráith na Ríg and may contain a burial or chambered tomb. The Lia Fáil, and the commemoration stone of the 1798 Battle of Tara, are now located on the Forradh.

The Lia Fáil, or crowning stone at Tara. It is thought the stone once stood at the entrance of the Mound of Hostages, and was removed to the Forradh later in history. Legend suggests, if the true king of Ireland gripped the stone, it would make an utterance, thereby confirming his status.

The Ráith of the Synods, a multi-vallate, ring barrow at Tara. This small ring barrow was nearly destroyed by British Israelites in the Victorian era, who excavated there, convinced the Ark of Covenant was buried somewhere within it.

The Rath of the Synods was built around the same time as the Ráith na Ríg. It is a much damaged multiple bank and fosse enclosure, with an incorporated barrow. It may have originally been a bowl barrow. It has been damaged over the centuries by church burials, the church wall, a townland boundary wall (since removed), and a misguided and messy excavation, by Victorian-era British Israelites, who thought the Ark of the Covenant was buried within it. Geophysical survey found that the Rath of the Synods was surrounded by a palisade and was associated with a flat cemetery, during the Iron Age. Evidence of a small, rectangular house was also found within the enclosure (Newman 1997: 225-230).

The final phase included the building of a massive palisade, on the interior of the Ráith na Ríg, and the construction of Tech Cormaic, a circular enclosure surrounded by a steep bank and ditch. It is the only true ring fort at the complex, and, though it is now joined to the Forradh, it was built at a later date. Other components of the Tara complex include, Ráith Lóegaire (Leary's Fort), a large (130 by 120m), circular bank and ditch enclosure, at the southern end of today's Tara landscape. Only part of it is visible today, due to farming activity. Two standing stones, in the courtyard of the church, have been incorporated into the Tara legends; they were to separate, for the rightful king's chariot when he approached the Hill. The Clóenfherta, or Sloping Trenches, located in the northwest of the site, are a complex series of ring barrows, which incorporate several smaller barrows into their structures. These enigmatic barrows are built onto the side of the Tara plateau and overlook the wide, Meath plains beyond. Ráith Gráinne may be a ring barrow and it is located to the north of the Ráith na Ríg, near the Clóenfherta. It is 70m in diameter, with a deep inner fosse and high bank. Geophysical survey has revealed several, now invisible, features in the field surrounding the Rath, including at least four additional barrows. Across the modern road, to the north, are a number of circular enclosures which were also likely part of the Tara complex (Newman 1995, 1997; Bhreathnach 1995, 1999; Fenwick and Newman 2002; Roche 2002).

The Iron Age components of the Hill of Tara, were constructed to be the focal point of royal ceremonial activity, for both Royal Mídh and later for the entire island. It is built on high ground, and is visible from many points in the old province. The Hill of Slane can be seen from Tara, along with many other sites across the Boyne Valley, making it an ideal defensive area as well. It is believed that the High Kings of Ireland, held ceremonies and seasonal gatherings at Tara and that they may have held, 'calls to arms', in times of conflict at the Hill. It is also felt, that people coming to Tara, may have entered by proceeding up the Banqueting Hall cursus. As one walks up the cursus today, the rest of the site remains invisible, until one reaches the crest of the hill, and can gaze out across the royal enclosure. In the Iron Age, visitors would have been able to walk directly toward the Rath of the Synods, Mound of Hostages, Tech Cormac, the Forradh, and the Lia Fáil, where it is believed the rulers of Ireland would have sat.

The conjoined Forradh (right), and Tech Cormaic (left) at Tara. Conjoined ring formations are considered to be indicative of 'royal sites' in Ireland.

The standing stones, located in the cemetery in the church grounds at Tara. The larger of the two, has a very degraded carving of a Sheela-na-Gig at its base. Legend suggests the stones would separate, when the rightful king would drive his chariot between them.

It is often hard to envision the activities, that would have taken place at Tara in the distant past, when visiting today. The site is quiet, often deserted, and lacks the over-marketed production of many of the other, arguably less important, sites in the country. Yet it is an astounding testament to the Irish people, who focussed their attention there from the Neolithic through the Iron Age. Intricately-constructed to take advantage of its particular environment, the site encompasses a wide, lifted plain roughly 2km long, which allows spectacular views of the surrounding landscape, especially that of Ireland's central plain to the west. None of the remaining components, give an indication that defence was the primary concern of the people who used Tara; rather, the site is constructed to impress upon visitors the importance of the location, and of the people who controlled it. Recent investigations, completed by Joe Fenwick, Conor Newman and The Discovery Programme, have shown Tara to be a much more complex site in the past. Great ditches, banks, palisaded enclosures, ring barrows, and other earthworks once cluttered the Tara cultural zone. This great concentration of sites within sites, and the astounding length of time in which the hill was in use (from roughly 5000 BCE through to AD 1100), give it the label of 'royal site'.

When visiting Tara, it is recommended that enough time be set aside to explore the site in its entirety. Visitors can take advantage of the small visitor's centre in St Patrick's church on the site, and can view the short twenty-five-minute film shown there. Entrance to the site is not controlled to any degree and there is no cost to visit unless the visitor's centre is used. Upon entering the site through the main gate, a large geophysical map of the site is located to the right, on the walkway leading to the visitor's centre. You must continue walking onto the site (either by the pathway near the Banqueting Hall, or through the cemetery near St Patrick's) in order to view all the components. The Hill of Tara is active farmland and often sheep will be grazing on it or farmers could be baling hay. It is not kept completely mown and can be slippery when the weather is inclement. It is recommended that proper footwear and rain gear be worn. The Hill of Tara is located off the N3/M3 north of Dublin. It is very well sign-posted and parking on all but the busiest days is adequate. There is also a cafe, gift shop and book shop located adjacent to the site.

*Rathcroghan Ceremonial Complex, County Roscommon*
The expansive landscape of Rathcroghan (also known as Crúachain Aí) in County Roscommon has been a focal point of cultural, ritual, and ceremonial activity

from the Neolithic period. The name Rathcroghan is used for both the large central mound located in Toberrory and for the surrounding ancient landscape. To differentiate between the two, I will refer to the landscape as Crúachain and the mound itself as Rathcroghan. The landscape itself is dotted with glacial ridges and drumlins (small hillocks), giving the pasturelands an undulating appearance. Many of the earthworks, mounds, and other ancient monuments have been constructed to take advantage of the natural landscape, resulting in many being visible for several miles. This high-ground visibility also causes many of the Crúachain monuments to be seen from the vantage point of the Rathcroghan mound.

Beginning in the early 1990s, the Department of Archaeology in the National University of Ireland, Galway, undertook a long-term geophysical study of the greater Crúachain landscape, including the Carnfree landscape, some 6km from the Rathcroghan mound. They found that the area had been first utilised by local populations in the Neolithic, beginning in around 3000 BCE, when they built at least one court tomb (now ruined), and some burial mounds. During the Bronze Age, after much forest clearance and the development of still visible field systems, further burial mounds were constructed. As the Bronze Age progressed, they shifted their preference from low-lying areas to the high ground, and built several more mounds, which would have been visible over wide distances. Waddell, Fenwick, and Barton remind us that assigning many of the sites to a particular period in the past is difficult, because so many of them were used over very long periods of time, and the entire landscape itself remained steeped in meaning for thousands of years (Waddell, Fenwick, Barton 2009). The many ring barrows in the complex are likely Bronze Age, but also could have been constructed and used into the Early Christian period. Rathcroghan mound itself seems to bridge the Late Bronze Age and Iron Age in terms of its construction and use. The mound itself may have been the ritual and inauguration site of the Connaught chieftains beginning in the Iron Age, and was likely the location of seasonal óenach, like Tailteann mentioned above.

Rathcroghan is an imposing, man-made earthen mound in the townland of Toberrory. It is approximately 88m in diameter and today rises to a height of about 6m above the present ground surface. There are two wide entrance ramps located on its eastern and western sides. Nearly invisible today is a 360m diameter bank, which encircles the mound. Within the enclosure are the fallen pillar stone known as Miosgan Meva, ring barrows, part of an ancient trackway, another round enclosure with an avenue north of the mound, parallel trenches which may have been an entrance trackway similar to the Banqueting Hall at Tara, as well as several other features, which are barely visible on the ground surface. The top of the large, flat-topped mound shows evidence of a double-walled enclosure (likely two separate building phases), and a small mound. There are also the remnants of two stone pillars located on the eastern and western ends of the mound. According to Waddell, Fenwick, and Barton, 'the great mound was both the focal monument of the entire Rathcroghan complex and the centrepiece within the large enclosure' (2009: 191). Many of the monuments of Crúachain are visible from the Rathcroghan mound.

Five hundred metres northeast of Rathcroghan is Rathbeg, a ring barrow on the summit of a natural drumlin, on a glacial ridge. It is about 40m in diameter and consists of a low grass mound, with two surrounding banks and internal ditches. Rathmore, about 900m from Rathcroghan, in the townland of Toberrory, is a large, raised ringfort and is likely medieval (Waddell, Fenwick, Barton 2009). It has an inner bank, set on a revetment of dry stone walling, and today, the broad southeastern entrance is still clear as it crosses the deep, wide fosse and low surrounding bank. Rathmore may have had a large palisaded structure, with an internal building on its summit, or possibly a timbered hall (Waddell, Fenwick, Barton 2009). Evidence suggests that Rathmore enjoyed long-term use.

The great ring fort of Ráth Mór located near Rathcroghan.

The massive, man–made mound of Rathcroghan, part of the Crúachain landscape in County Roscommon. Rathcroghan is associated with the epic Táin bó Cúailgne and Queen Medb of Connaught.

The entrance to Oweynagat Cave. The cave is believed to be the entrance to the underworld, home of the Tuatha de Danann.

In Glenballythomas, the great ringed enclosure of Rathnadarve is visible. It is a huge structure with a single high bank, and exterior ditch of 115m diameter enclosing a low glacial hillock. Nearby, are the nearly invisible 250m enclosure, and the mythical Oweynagat Cave ('Cave of the Cat'). Oweynagat is a natural underground limestone cave, which today is entered through a later souterrain marked by a low lintel. In early literature it is known as the entrance to the Otherworld. Presently, the cave is only about 50m long, due to road construction which bisected the interior causing it to end abruptly. The cave has likely been used for a variety of ceremonial uses for many thousands of years. Remnants of a ringed structure have been discovered near the entrance, and Ogham inscriptions are visible on the lintels which relate the cave to Fraech, one of the participants in the Cattle Raid of Cooley instigated by Queen Medb in the Iron Age. The inscription has been interpreted as '*VRAICCI ... MAQI MEDVVI* (Fraech, son of Medb).'

Further along and south of Rathcroghan, in Glenballythomas, are the Mucklaghs, two enormous banked earthworks. The northern Mucklagh is a massive double-banked structure resembling a droveway, about 100m long. The southern Mucklagh runs nearly 280m long. These huge earthworks run northeast-southwest, must have served a ceremonial purpose, and would probably have been a multi-period monument. Not far from the Mucklaghs are Relignaree, a large, circular earthen enclosure, once thought to be the burial place of the pagan kings of Ireland, and Daithi's Mound, a smaller ring barrow with a central pillar stone. Daithi's Mound is the mythological burial mound of the last pagan king of Ireland, but there is no archaeological evidence to substantiate this.

Roughly six kilometres from the Rathcroghan mound, is the Carnfree complex, a densely-populated landscape of eleven burial mounds, three standing stones, several enclosures, and ancient field systems. This grouping of archaeological features also seems to be both spatially and temporally related to the archaeological landscape of Rathcroghan mound and Crúachain.

Crúachain has remained in Irish consciousness because of its relationship to the tales of the Táin bó Cúailgne, and its later connection to the O'Connor sept, who were a powerful ruling family in the area through the medieval period. This extraordinary landscape must be seen to be fully appreciated. It is recommended that visitors begin at the Crúachain Aí Centre in Tulsk, where staff will guide you through the informative exhibits on this complex landscape. Rathcoghan mound is north of Tulsk and, like all the monuments of the Crúachain and Carnfree landscapes, is located on private farmland. Exercise caution when entering the site, because cattle or sheep could be grazing nearby and electric fencing is in use. Please also remember to close and lock all gates you open. Rathbeg is slightly further north and can be seen from the great mound of Rathcroghan. Rathmore is also on the road running north from Tulsk and can be seen on the right-hand side, across from a small national school. Rathnadarve is located on the right, on the small secondary road running west by Rathbeg; further along this road, you must turn left onto a tertiary road to go to Oweynagat Cave. Daithi's Mound, Relignaree, and the Mucklaghs are only accessible by walking across the fields adjacent to Oweynagat Cave. You must wear appropriate clothing when entering the cave, as it is always wet and muddy. You must also bring a torch or headlamp. It is not recommended that you enter the cave alone, if you do not have a light source, or if you suffer from claustrophobia, as it is a very small, dark, enclosed space, and is not easy to get out of once you slide down through the souterrain to the cave entrance.

*Above:* One of the Ogham script inscriptions on a lintel in the entance to Oewynagat Cave, which makes reference to Fraech, son of Maeve (photo courtesy Jessica Guertin ©).

*Right:* The natural limstone fissure of Oweynagat Cave (photo courtesy Jessica Guertin ©).

A view from the medieval souterrain, which is used as the modern entrance to the cave (photo courtesy of Jessica Guertin).

*The Navan Complex, Armagh, County Armagh*

To the north, the great Navan Fort rises on a natural drumlin, near the city of Armagh. Part of an expansive, ceremonial landscape which includes the Bronze Age Haughey's Fort, the man-made ritual pond of the King's Stables, and Loughnashade, Navan Fort (or Emain Macha) was once the seat of the powerful kings of Ulster (the Ulaid) and the later great Uí Neill. Surrounded by massive multiple banks and ditches, the fort looms above the landscape. At the apex of the drumlin, the remains of an enormous 40-metre span structure testifies to the incredible importance of the site. Like Tara, Navan has been in use since the Neolithic. The remains of hearths, houses, and stone tools were found beneath the mound during excavations by Dudley Waterman and Christopher Lynn in the 1960s and '70s, but it is in the Irish Iron Age that the site emerges as the centre of power for the tribes of Ulster. Among the finds discovered at Navan, was the skull of a Barbary ape, thought to have been a gift to the territory's ruler from another powerful group on the Barbary Coast. This artefact alone suggests that the people of Emain Macha had trade contacts reaching far and wide. The 40m structure excavated by Waterman and Lynn, was filled with stones and ritually burnt sometime around the birth of Christ. This may symbolise either a shift in power, or the movement of the centre of ritual and kingship to another site.

The Hill of Tara, Crúachain, and Navan Fort are three of the four major Iron Age 'royal sites' in Ireland (the fourth is Dún Ailinne in Kildare). They are all integral parts of Ireland's legendary past, and all are mentioned in several early Irish epics, the most well-known being the Táin bó Cúailgne mentioned above in reference to Rathcroghan. In the Táin, Queen Medb's lust for the Brown Bull of Cooley brings about a fierce, prolonged war with the Red Branch Knights of Navan Fort. Navan was ruled by King Conchobar mac Nessa and among his knights was the great hero, Cúchulainn, a feared and powerful warrior, who was the son of the god Lugh. The lands around Navan Fort are where the Red Branch Knights and the boy troops would have trained and practised their battle tactics. It was from Navan Fort that King Conchobar mac Nessa sent his armies into battle against the armies of Connaught.

The mound which covers the forty-metre structure at Navan Fort (Emain Macha), in Armagh, Northern Ireland.

The low exterior bank which surrounds the forty-metre structure at Navan Fort.

The site of Navan Fort is an impressive 250m diameter bank and ditched enclosure, that is built on a natural glacial drumlin, less than two miles (1.6km) west of the city of Armagh. It is an unusual structure because the deep ditch is inside the bank rather than outside and, on the western half of the site, is the large 40m mound, which covers the remnant of the huge structure built in around 93BCE. This enormous structure is thought to have been used for ceremonial purposes, though what those ceremonies may have been we cannot be sure. It may be that Navan was used in the same ways as Tara and Rathcroghan; as the seat of the ruling chieftain, a gathering place for the local tribes, for the planning and executing of raids and battles, as a training ground for warriors, and as a location for the óenach.

The very deep fosse and high surrounding banks at Navan Fort.

When Navan Fort was excavated by Dudley Waterman and Christopher Lynn in the 1970s (Christopher Lynn and others continue to actively investigate the Navan Complex of sites today), they were surprised to find that the 40m mound contained the remains of the structure mentioned above. They found that the building was round, and had been constructed in such a way that it needed a huge tree trunk (the base of which was recovered) to hold up a massive, conical thatched roof. A structure of this size would not have been used as a home, though this does not mean it was not occupied. This building is believed to have been a focal point of the surrounding countryside, and used as both a ceremonial and administrative centre for the territory during the Iron Age. Of particular interest, is the fact that shortly after the building was constructed, it was filled with stones and ritually, burned before being covered with turf and soil as we see it today (Waterman 1997).

The great outer bank and ditch, also enclose a visible Bronze Age ring barrow to the east of the interior mound. Geophysical survey and excavation have revealed that this ring barrow conjoins another, now invisible barrow, constructed some time prior to the ring barrow. Excavations by Waterman and Lynn also revealed the remains of Neolithic habitation underneath the mound. Like Tara to the south, Navan Fort was a well-known focus of prehistoric activity from the Stone Age, through the Iron Age, and into the historic period.

Further to the west, is the enigmatic site of the King's Stables, an artificial pond built during the Bronze Age. It was named the King's Stables in later history, because local people believed the kings of the Ulaid, and later Úi Neill, would stable and bathe their horses there. No evidence exists in the archaeology to support this. Rather, Christopher Lynn excavated a very small portion of the pond in the 1970s and found it to be a man-made pool with steep sides, high banks, and a very flat bottom. Even though his excavation was limited, he recovered hundreds of artefacts, animal remains and part of a human skull (see Chapter 4). A few hundred metres west of the King's Stables, is the Bronze Age Haughey's Fort, a large triple bank and ditch ring fort that likely served a ceremonial as well as habitation purpose for the people of the area. Haughey's Fort and the King's Stables appear to have been in use at the same time (Lynn 2003).

Slightly north-east of Navan Fort, is Loughnashade, a natural deep pool that was used by Bronze and Iron Age people for votive offerings. Votive offerings are artefacts that have been ritually deposited, usually in water, as a gift to the gods. The lake has not been fully examined, but in the past, several bronze ceremonial horns and other artefacts have been discovered at Loughnashade. Today, the body of water known as Loughnashade is a small portion of what it was in the Iron Age when the people of Navan Fort would have visited it.

The Iron Age in Ireland, despite its ambiguous beginnings, lasted much longer than it did in most other areas of Europe. It was not until the coming of Christianity in the fifth century, that the strong tribal culture of the Iron Age began to change. The provincial centres of power gradually weakened, the villages surrounding them developed their own systems of leadership which became more and more centred on the Church, and the tribalism so prevalent for so many centuries, began to evolve into the parishes recognised today.


## THE CELTIC QUESTION

Inevitably, in any discussion of the Iron Age or of Ireland, there arises the question of the people known as the Celts. Who were the Celts? Where did they come from? What do they mean in regard to European prehistory?

The Celts have long been thought to have been the major contributors to the development of the European Iron Age. In the late 1800s, Georg Ramsaur excavated the site of Hallstatt in Austria, and recognised the archaeological remains there as 'Celtic'. The Greeks had written of a people to the north whom they called Keltoi, and the Romans also wrote of northern peoples they called the Galatae, who are believed to have been the same people. The Hallstatt-C and -D eras, or early Iron Age, lasted from around 800-450 BCE. The La Téne period developments which followed, were understood as a further cultural evolution of those begun by the Hallstatt people. The people who crossed through Europe, faced Caesar, and put Rome to the torch, were also called the Celts by later investigators. In the Victorian era, a great 'Celtic Revival' began which, in many ways, invented a common culture, language, and ancestry for the great peoples of Victorian Europe. Today there is substantial debate regarding the Celts among the archaeological community. What is known in Ireland, is that there is no evidence of a large invasion of people in the Iron Age, nor of any profound cultural changes at about the time things were shifting, due to immigration in other areas of Europe. The Irish Iron Age is essentially Ireland's own creation, with little influence from the outside world. The Celts, such as they were, never arrived in any great numbers to Ireland's shores, nor did they mould Irish culture.

## THE END OF PREHISTORY IN IRELAND

In the fifth century, Ireland witnessed a sea change, when a small contingent of believers in a young religion, landed on its shores. Christianity was to alter the course of Irish history in a way nothing before, or since, has. In this relatively bloodless revolution, men like St Patrick, St Columba, and St Ciaran appealed to the tribes, by showing them parallels between the two belief systems. Soon the great tribal centres of power were usurped by the peaceful establishment of centres of worship and 'white martyrdom' (self-imposed isolation). The monastic groups which formed, recorded the stories and legends of the Irish peoples (such as the Táin mentioned above), and, while the rest of Europe languished in the Dark Ages after the fall of Rome, they established schools and centres of learning throughout Ireland, and eventually Europe. The coming of the Cross marks the end of ancient Ireland, and the dawning of a new day in the history of the island and the Irish people.

# BIBLIOGRAPHY

Bhreathnach, E., 'The Tara Project: The topography of Tara: The documentary evidence' pp. 68-76 *Discovery Programme Report* (2) (1995).

Bhreathnach, E., 'Authority and Supremacy in Tara and its Hinterlands c. 950-1200' pp. 1-24 *Discovery Programme Report* (5) (1999).

Bergh, S., 'Knocknarea: The ultimate monument: Megaliths and mountain in Neolithic Cúil Irra, north-west Ireland' pp. 139-151, in Scarre, C. (ed) *Monuments and Landscape in Atlantic Europe* (Routedge: London, 2002).

Fenwick, J., & Newman, C., 'Geomagnetic Survey in the Hill of Tara Co. Meath 1998-9' pp. 1-18 *Discovery Programme Report* (6) (2002).

Harbison, P., *Pre-Christian Ireland: From the First Settlers to the Early Celts* (Thames and Hudson: London, 1988).

Herity, M., & Eogan G., *Ireland in Prehistory* (Routledge: London, 1977).

Kenny, N,. (unpub. ms.) Wood charring and fuel production in early medieval and late medieval Ireland—revelations from recent excavations.

Kristiansen, K., & Larsson, T.B., *The Rise of Bronze Age Society: Travels, transmissions and transformations*, (Cambridge University Press: Cambridge, 2005).

Lynn, C., 'A Burnt Layer Inside the King's Stables' pp. 41-2, *Emania* (8) (1991).

Lynn, C., *Navan Fort: Archaeology and Myth* (Wordwell: Bray, 2003).

Mallory, J.P., & McNeill, T.E., *The Archaeology of Ulster: From colonization to plantation* (Belfast: Queen's University: Belfast, 1991).

Malone, C., *Neolithic Britain and Ireland* (Tempus: Stroud 2001).

Newman, C., *Tara: An archaeological survey* (Royal Irish Academy: Dublin, 1997).

O'Brien, W., *Mount Gabriel: Bronze Age Mining in Ireland* (Galway University Press: Galway, 1994).

O'Brien, W., *Bronze Age Copper Mining in Britain and Ireland* (Princes: Rosborough, 1996).

O'Brien, W., 'Megaliths in a mythologised landscape: South-west Ireland in the Iron Age' pp. 152-176, in Scarre, C. (ed) *Monuments and Landscape in Atlantic Europe* (Routledge: London, 2002).

O'Kelly, M., *Newgrange: Archaeology, Art and Legend*, (Thames and Hudson: London, 1982).

O'Kelly, M., *Early Ireland: An Introduction to Irish Prehistory*, (Cambridge University Press: Cambridge, 1989).

Roche, H., 'Excavations at Ráith na Ríg, Tara, Co. Meath 1997' pp. 19-82, *Discovery Programme Report* (6) (2002).

Sahlins, M., *Stone Age Economics*, (Chicago: Aldine-Atherton, 1971).

Stout, G., *Newgrange and the Bend of the Boyne*, (Cork University Press: Cork, 2002).

Thorpe, N., 'Origins of War: Mesolithic conflict in Europe' *British Archaeology* (52) (2000) online version (www.britarch.ac.uk/ba/ba52/ba52feat.html).

Waddell, J., *The Prehistoric Archaeology of Ireland*, (Wordwell: Bray, 2000).

Waddell, J., Fenwick, J., and Barton, K., *Rathcroghan: Archaeological and Geophysical Survey in a Ritual Landscape*, (Wordwell: Bray, 2009).

Waterman, D., & Lynn C., *Excavations at Navan Fort 1961-71*, (Stationery Office: Belfast 1997).